Shepherd
Warrior

D1527999

Shepherd
Warrior

Ulrich Zwingli

William Boekestein

CF4·K

10 9 8 7 6 5 4 3 2 1

Copyright © 2016 William Boekestein

Paperback ISBN: 978-1-78191-803-6

epub ISBN: 978-1-78191-879-1

mobi ISBN: 978-1-78191-880-7

Published by Christian Focus Publications,
Geanies House, Fearn, Tain, Ross-shire,
IV20 1TW, Scotland, U.K.
www.christianfocus.com; email: info@christianfocus.com

Cover design by Daniel van Straaten
Cover illustration by Jeff Anderson
Printed and bound by Nørhaven, Denmark
American English is used throughout this book

While imagination has crafted many of the scenes and conversations
between the characters of this book, they are based on significant
historical research and reflect the true story of Ulrich Zwingli's life. All
of the letters and most of the longer speeches of Zwingli (and many of
the shorter ones) are adaptations from original records. Zwingli's poem
in chapter three and song in chapter eleven are fresh paraphrases by
the author. Students interested in a more detailed account of Zwingli's
life are encouraged to read the author's *Ulrich Zwingli* (EP Books, 2015
ISBN: 978-1-78397-082-7).

Zwingli's song on page 122 comes from the Moravian Book of Worship
#760.

Contents

To Asher, Evangelia, Mina,
and Hazel
(Psalm 127:4)

The Birth of a Warrior

The first rays of the morning sun filtered through dew-laden pine trees, and between the stone and wood buildings surrounding the city square called "Charity." Typically, the square came to life gradually, the way a person likes to wake up on a weekend. But on this early morning, the usually quiet streets teemed with life. The crisp air resonated with the mingled sounds of shuffling leather, jangling steel, and whinnying horses—all of which aroused the curiosity and anxiety of the town dogs, who added their voices to the melee. Thousands of boots clomped their way through the narrow, winding streets. The boots were worn by men donning the best military equipment they could muster on short notice—thus the jangling steel. Most of the bearded, rough-looking men carried pikes—spear-tipped sturdy poles easily three times as tall as the men who carried them. The pikemen also carried either halberds—a cross between a staff and an ax—or longswords, both of which would be used in close, hand-to-hand combat.

The previous night, alarm bells had pealed from every tower in the canton, or state, of Zurich, Switzerland, beginning at the center of the capital city with the same name. A volunteer army began to assemble to halt the advancing enemy. At full daylight, the city streets resembled what happens moments after a curious boy disrupts an enormous ant hill. Some of the citizen-soldiers raced to the city arms locker to find weapons. Others, increasingly clustering into small groups, returned with what weapons they could find. Their faces showed warrior determination, even if their hearts were filled with fear of the unknown. Most of the activity led to various cobblestone squares where small bands formed into larger ones. Between the bands of men, roamed horses, their hooves clattering at the prodding of their riders. Cannon, borne on iron-reinforced wooden wheels, bounced rhythmically along the stone streets.

Army captains, who had only recently been given marching orders, desperately lobbed commands into the mounting confusion.

"Men, we must march!" The company commander— also the town butcher—turned on his heels toward the rising sun and marched down the steep alley that led to the narrow, northern tip of Lake Zurich.

As if on cue, the solid wooden door of the stone house that still cast a shrinking shadow on the remaining soldiers swung open. Three children tumbled down the steps and sped toward the curly-

8

red-haired man who was dismounting his horse to meet their embrace.

"Papa! Don't go, Papa!" Seven-year-old Regula struggled to catch her breath after blurting out the words between violent sobs. William and young Ulrich, two and four years younger than their sister, nearly knocked her over as they flew to clasp their father's legs.

The soldier, a minister by calling, removed his helmet to look into his children's faces one last time. For nearly the first time since meeting each of his children on the days of their birth, the preacher was lost for words. As he looked up to gather his thoughts, and be relieved of the unbearable pain etched in his children's faces, the door of his house opened a few more inches. His "two Annas" seemed to glide toward him without touching the ground, wrapped in a cream-colored shawl. His baby, only a year old, squirmed in her mother's arms, her face set between a smile and a scream. His wife wore a similar expression.

"Goodbye, Ulrich ..." she started, then faltered. She bit her quivering lip. Her eyes squeezed shut, as if to block out the painful scene.

Ulrich scooped up Regula and nearly dragged his sons on his legs to cover the last few paces that separated himself from his bride of only seven years. For a second, the confusing scene that had been swirling around the family seemed to freeze as they locked their heaving bodies.

Everyone waited for the father to speak.

"The hour has come that separates us. Let it be. It is God's will." He tightened his arms as emotion tightened his throat.

The words of her pastor, and spiritual friend, strengthened Anna. "We shall all see each other again if it is God's will." Thinking of the children, she added, "And what will you bring back when you come?"

"A blessing after the dark night," he answered.

Ulrich pressed his family to his heart for as long as he dared. As he pulled away, he forced his best smile before donning his helmet to shroud his tears and his contorted face. As horse and rider turned the corner of the street, Ulrich turned back for one last look and a wave.

Regula broke free of her mother's arms. Her father cringed at the sight of her tear-soaked face and wriggling lips. He turned his face away just before her shrill voice pierced through the noise of the crowd.

"PAPA!"

Over and over, the word rattled in his brain as his broad-sword rattled at his side.

"Papa! Papa!"

Tears began to blur Ulrich's vision as his mind drifted from the image of Regula's pleading face to an image of his own pleading face, from a day nearly fifty years earlier.

* * *

"Papa, I'm scared." Five-year old Ulrich Zwingli's voice was barely audible. His damp face was buried deep in his father's leather jerkin.

Ulrich's father and namesake reassured his third child. "Son, you'll only be a day's hike away and Uncle Bartholomew will take good care of you."

"But why can't I stay here with you and Mama and everyone?" Ulrich stammered. As the boy turned his face toward his mother, his father quickly wiped away the tear that was gathering on his own eyelid.

"You're too smart to live in this tiny village. Besides, do you always want to be outnumbered by sheep and cows?" his father offered, trying to force a laugh.

It was nearly impossible for Ulrich to imagine living anywhere other than in the rustic village of Wildhaus, Switzerland, surrounded by the massive foothills of the Swiss Alps. Life in Wildhaus was good, especially for the Zwinglis. The senior Ulrich was the chief magistrate of the village, earning him a good living and the respect of all his peers.

From the front of their home Ulrich could watch the young men, including his older brothers Henry and Nicholas, drive the cattle and herds from their winter grazing grounds in the valley to the tops of the surrounding peaks in the warmer months. Only in summer were the sun's rays powerful enough to sprout grass in the highlands. The animals' bells rang as gently and steadily as the brook that ran between the mountains. As a young child, Ulrich often lost himself in thought and song in the meadows around his house.

The Zwingli home was better than most. Still, his large family—several more children followed after him—lived snugly in a small log home with wooden shingles held down with rocks to protect against the intense winter winds that ripped between mountain ridges. In the glow of the kitchen fire, Ulrich and his siblings often listened to their father talk politics, religion, and history.

"Boys," he would say, "Did I ever tell you about the time that your grandfather shot an apple off my head with his crossbow?"

"Papa," crowed the boys, politely rolling their eyes, "Grandpa wasn't William Tell."

"Ah, so you've heard of him, have you?" grinned the elder Ulrich as he took a slow draught from a mug of apple ale. "It was about 200 years ago. Our confederacy was as young as I am now—though not half as strong."

The boys grinned.

"But already, the future of our cantons was unsure. The Habsburg Empire was breathing down our necks, threatening our independence. One foreign overlord raised a pole in one of our villages, placed his hat on it, and required everyone to bow to it." Their father leaned forward, elbows on his knees, and stared intently from one son's face to another. As the tension built, he slammed his fist on the table. "But the Swiss bow before no one!" he shouted.

"This was just what William Tell said to his boy as they strolled through the village together one fine afternoon. He refused to bow and was bound with ropes in consequence. Knowing the stories about Tell's near-magical powers with the cross bow, the Habsburg judge gave the punishment: 'You can escape my sword if you shoot an arrow off your son's head!' Tell was good, like all Swiss men should be, but just in case, he drew two bolts from his quiver. 'The second's for you, if the first flies untrue,' he hissed in the direction of the judge."

For effect, the storyteller placed an apple on young Ulrich's head and reenacted Tell's perfect shot, sending the apple flying with a thrust from the tip of a powerful finger. The boys cheered.

If he stayed in Wildhaus, Ulrich could grow up to drive cattle, log timber, or build furniture. Or, like William Tell, he could become a soldier. The trouble was in those days, most Swiss soldiers fought for the glory of killing and the gold of foreign kings, not to defend their homeland. As a local official, Ulrich's father had surely observed the steady incline of demand for Swiss fighters, especially from the French. Young Ulrich had also often heard him discussing with his uncle the negative impact of mercenary soldiering. While experienced Swiss warriors returned home with stories of valor and handsome rewards, the soldier's life often led to moral degradation. Ulrich had once overheard his father and mother talking. "Young Ulrich is gifted, dear," his father had said. "Perhaps he will be a different kind of warrior. Maybe he will fight evil with words." His mother had said nothing; she only offered her husband a lip-bitten smile.

"Well, my boy, your bag is packed with enough cheese and bread to get you to Weesen. Provided…" Ulrich's father cleared his throat and glanced playfully at his brother, "provided you can keep the bag away from Uncle Bartholomew."

"A teacher has to be paid somehow!" replied Bartholomew, as he stooped to grab his own bag. He rejoined his staff, which he had leaned against the house upon entering. As the boy turned to follow, his mother dropped to her knees on the rough wooden floor; her strong arms said what her tear-choked voice could not.

Young Ulrich raised himself to the extent of his little frame and offered—in the manliest voice he could muster, "I'll be all right, I promise."

"With God's help, you will be," said his father. "But just to be sure, I'll go with you a few steps."

"If you do become a scholar," Ulrich overheard him whisper, "it'll be too seldom that we see our boy in this humble countryside."

The Shaping of a Scholar-Shepherd

Six-year-old Ulrich swung his feet beneath the crude pine bench in his Uncle Bartholomew's simple log cabin. The small window in the rough wooden wall behind him kept out most of the sunlight—the many gaps in the chinking between the wooden beams let in enough sound to distract all but the most serious of students. Birds chattered and sung in the pine forest outside. Working boys laughed and whistled as they drove their herds and flocks between the woods from the fields to the ten-mile-long Walen Lake. The early morning sun danced playfully on the waves.

Two other students, both older and rather average, sat on the same bench, one on Ulrich's right, the other on his left. The scrawny boy to the right was an orphan who somehow managed to pay for his education by yodeling in the city square in front of a crude wooden box: "My pantry, wardrobe, bank, and library, rolled into one," he called it. Tips had been sparse lately; his stomach rumbled noisily. On Ulrich's left sat the stout son of a local cattle trader, carelessly doodling on his slate with a bit of chalk.

Though still a novice, in his first year of schooling Ulrich had gained a passion for learning. He hung on Bartholomew's every word; he would have to if he hoped to learn anything. Unlike schools in larger cities, where books and paper were more plentiful, the library of the little private school in Weesen contained only a few tattered volumes. Ulrich was beginning to build a library in his own mind, storing the words he heard in just the right places, and quickly grabbing them off the shelf when necessary.

"We will begin the day with the prayer of Bruder Klaus," announced the teacher. "Who can recite it for us?"

The yodeler began carefully studying his ragged leather shoes, as if too busy to be called upon. The other boy inhaled sharply as he scrunched up his face and scratched his curly blonde hair. He seemed to be working hard to give the impression that the answer was on the tip of his tongue.

Ulrich closed his eyes for a moment before rising to his feet, his eyes still gently pressed tight in concentration. "My Lord and my God, take from me everything that distances me from you. My Lord and my God, give me everything that brings me closer to you. My Lord and my God, detach me from myself to give my all to you."

So began another of the thousand school days Ulrich spent in Weesen, which consisted of studying the Latin Vulgate Bible and other religious classics.

On one of these days, Bartholomew pressed the class. "Please identify the three principles or beginnings of Aristotle with which Lombard begins his Sentences."

At the word "Aristotle", Ulrich flicked from his palm a squashed mosquito and looked curiously at his uncle. "Do you mean Plato, Uncle?"

"Yes, of course, I was only testing you," said Uncle Bartholomew; his eyes glanced uneasily at the other students.

"Ulrich, come with me." Bartholomew ducked to clear the low cabin door. Outside, he continued, "You are doing very well in your studies. To be quite honest, I'm no longer the best teacher for you. I promised your father I'd help you become a scholar. And I've done my best, but you need a better school. You need to go to Basel."

Basel opened a whole new world to the young scholar. For the first time, he was able to interact with other students who also treasured learning.

He was particularly enamored with the newly fashionable discipline of debate. He listened intently while his teacher, Master Buenzli, a distant relative, explained the power of persuasion.

"Never underestimate the strength of a good argument. It is no wonder that King Solomon said, 'By long forbearance a ruler is persuaded, and a gentle tongue breaks a bone.'[1] God endowed his creatures

---

1. Proverbs 25:15.

with divine rationality. If you can learn from Aristotle to master the skills of persuasion, language, and logical arrangements, you will be more powerful than Augustus."

"What could I do for God," wondered Ulrich, "If I could help people see right from wrong by clear logic?"

While workmen methodically chiseled the red sandstone pieces that were being fitted into the slender tower of the impressive Romanesque cathedral on the Rhine River, Ulrich chiseled away at his speeches until they were beautiful, sound, and persuasive. He dreamed of standing in front of sprawling audiences, quoting word-for-word from the classic writers, all the while gazing intently into the faces of his fixated listeners. His last line, a daring taunt to his would-be challenges, would be, "If I have misspoken, stand up and speak in the name of God. Here I am!"

Ulrich's dream was hardly interrupted by the rhythmic thuds of the professor's footsteps as he paced between the aisles of students.

"But before any of you will become a Pericles," the professor's voice trilled as he pronounced the name of the famous Greek orator, "you must devote yourself to learning." The professor then tapped, with his wooden pointer, on the top of the dreamy boy's wavy reddish-brown hair. "Books must be your best friends, words your greatest joy, and your mind and heart your most powerful tools."

That night, with his teacher's speech still ringing in his ears, Ulrich penned a letter to his father. "Father, with God's help, one day I'll become an orator. Master Buenzli has inspired me. He's also encouraged me to study under a true lover of words, a poet. He suggested Heinrich Woelfli of Berne. I hope you will consent to my transfer."

Soon Ulrich was on his way to the neighboring canton of Berne.

Not only was Master Woelfli a distinguished poet, he was also a noted singer. Words flew almost magically from his pen and his mouth. While in Berne, Ulrich's own musical talents were quickly noticed by the religious order of the Dominicans.

"You sing like a song thrush," one friar told him. "Your voice is agreeable and melodious. It isn't strong, but it goes straight to the heart. You have all the makings of a gospel troubadour. Join our order; become a Dominican monk."

Excitedly, Ulrich wrote to his father about this fascinating opportunity. "And just think," he concluded, "I'll be sleeping out under the starry sky, trading sermon and song for my supper—isn't it exciting, Papa?"

The last thing Ulrich senior wanted for his gifted son of thirteen years was to be traveling the countryside with itinerant preachers, begging for food, selling his voice for clothes. The next thing Ulrich knew, his uncle Bartholomew was helping him pack his few belongings into a leather satchel. Ulrich was off to another school— this time, much further from home.

"Surgite discipuli!" The Viennese schoolmaster's Latin words echoed into the bare classroom a split second before his grim face peered through the doorway. Already Ulrich and his fellow classmates were standing to attention.

In perfect unison, the students responded with the expected Latin greeting, *"Salve Magister."*

Ulrich stole a quick glance at his new friend Joachim Vadian. Both friends knew what the other was thinking. Their instructors seemed to love making their students squirm by requiring them to speak Latin at all times. When some of the boys were out of the earshot of their masters, they chattered amongst themselves in their native German. But Ulrich and Joachim had found a new love in the old language of Rome. They read Latin books, composed Latin poems, and sang Latin songs—even in their meager free time.

Although class time sped by quickly for the young scholar, Ulrich eagerly awaited dismissal. As the red rays of the setting sun shimmered between the roofs of the university buildings, Ulrich's fingers affectionately smoothed the curling edges of the worn leather book that sat on his desk, drawing Joachim's attention. Joachim smiled. As soon as class was over, his friend would become lost in another world, the world of Greek mythology.

"Ulrich!"

The young man flinched only slightly at the sound of his name as he stood at his desk in front of the now-dark window, overlooking the slender alley below. The candle on his desk flickered wildly whenever the young scholar exhaled. His wide eyes were buried in his warped leather book. His mind and heart had been carried 1,300 hundred miles south, and thousands of mythical years earlier.

"No one must ever see him and live to tell about it Daedalus," demanded the king.

Daedalus, the Athenian inventor, had built an intricate maze called a labyrinth, designed to hide the monstrous Minotaur son of Minos, the ruler of Crete. The Minotaur's appetite for human flesh was satisfied by the offering of seven young men and women of Athens, once every seven years. One year, one of the victims was a young warrior named Theseus. After one look at the Athenian, Ariadne – Minos' daughter – had fallen in love.

"Daedalus," whispered Ariadne, "you must help me save Theseus." Sensing his hesitation, Ariadne added, "How can you bear to see one of your own native brothers thrown to that monster?"

Reluctantly, Daedalus offered his advice. "Conceal a ball of thread in Theseus' shirt, and hide a dagger in the labyrinth. He must tie the thread near the opening of the maze to help him find his way back, or he'll never escape."

Thus equipped, Theseus began tediously weaving his way closer to the center of the maze toward the terrifying screams of the Minotaur. At last, a single wall of chiseled stone separated man from beast. Heavy sweat began to bead on Theseus' forehead as he drew his dagger from its sheath. Four more steps and the Minotaur's burning red eyes locked relentlessly on the man; the beast lowered his shoulders and began to charge.

"Ulrich!" This time the voice was accompanied by a piece of chalk that glanced harmlessly off the young man's back.

"What was that for?"

"I couldn't get your attention," replied Joachim. "That old book enchants you!"

"Joachim, aren't you captivated by the courage, wisdom, and commitment to justice that God gave to the Greeks? When I picture Theseus slaying the Minotaur and freeing his friends from the labyrinth, I feel like I could be just as heroic for God."

"Well, hero," joked Joachim, "It's time to study physics, so you'll need to be more like the scientist Daedalus than the soldier Theseus."

Ulrich's two years in Vienna strengthened his love for ancient learning. His approach to school work was nearly relentless, though he did carve out time to make music, honing his skill on several woodwinds and stringed instruments. Over the years, he had learned to play ten musical instruments in all. Music always reminded Ulrich of home, the place where his heart first skipped to the sound of the dulcimer and where his spirit soared as song echoed between mountain ridges. Increasingly, his heart tugged less for home, and more for further learning.

In his eighteenth year, Ulrich returned to Basel to finish his classical studies. This time, as an educated young man, he supported himself and paid for his education by teaching Latin.

In Basel, Ulrich's unquestioning support of the Roman Catholic Church, the only church he and his classmates had ever known, came under pressure.

"Have you heard," quipped his respected teacher Thomas Wyttenbach, "that our 'Holy Father' has once again become a 'grandfather?'"

Awkward laughter cackled around the room.

Everyone in Wyttenbach's class was aware of two awkward facts. The first was that the Pope was to set an example of celibacy; he and other ordained churchmen were not allowed to marry so that they might practice singular devotion to God. The second was that sexual immorality among the clergy was rampant. The current Pope, Alexander VI, had several known mistresses and openly acknowledged their children as his.

"Show me from Scripture," continued the teacher, "where priests are forbidden to marry or allowed to have mistresses. While we're at it, show me where God gives absolute spiritual power to the Pope, including the power to forgive sin through the sale of paper indulgences."

As the teacher went on, the snickering stopped. Pious students began nervously scratching on their papers with dry quills.

"I'm not questioning the church," Wyttenbach assured the students. "I'm only asking questions."

These were questions that Ulrich would soon be forced to consider. Not long after graduating as a Master of Arts, Ulrich was asked to pastor a small Catholic Church in the little town of Glarus, just a day's hike from his childhood home.

Field Preacher

A dozen wooden tankards of beer sat upon a rough wooden table. Affixed to most of the tankards was a hardened hand of a working man of Glarus. Every so often, a tankard traveled slowly to a bearded face that showed the signs of deep thought.

"He's a bit young, isn't he?" questioned one of the men.

"He's young," replied another, quickly, "but he's bright, kind, and energetic. More than that, when he speaks, he sounds like one of us, not like a talking book from a strange place."

"Besides," added a third man, "I don't care for an Italian telling us who will be priest in Glarus, even if that Italian is the Pope."

Grunts of agreement sounded from around the table.

Thus, it was settled. Twenty-two-year-old Ulrich Zwingli would become priest of the small Swiss town of Glarus. Ulrich was ordained by Bishop Hugo of Constance, and performed his first Mass in his home church which had been built around the time of his birth. Ulrich's father was pleased. His efforts to educate his son had paid off. But not everyone was pleased. Henry Goldli was the man whom the Pope had approved to become the priest of Glarus. Goldli refused to renounce his claim to the post until Ulrich agreed to pay him an annual stipend.

As an energetic priest, Ulrich began, as expected, to study, preach and teach. He often buried his head for hours in ancient writings, both Christian and heathen. But the young priest could not escape a crisis that pressed upon his heart with growing weight. Young men from his own parish, and across the Swiss confederacy, were selling themselves as mercenaries— soldiers serving foreign armies in exchange for pay.

While making his rounds throughout the village, Ulrich couldn't help but notice the negative effects of this mercenary trafficking. He could hardly make his way from the rectory to the market without passing a maimed veteran shaking a wooden cup and begging for bread. He had heard the sobs of enough widows whose husbands had been cut down on foreign soil. Soldiers who returned safely from battle usually returned with large salaries. They also imported bad habits. Three years after Ulrich's ordination, the Swiss people had entered into a five year pact to provide soldiers to defend the interests of Rome in foreign wars.

Standing in front of his writing desk, Ulrich took a deep breath as he remembered the thoughts that swirled through his mind as he took his priestly vows: "The blood of the sheep, who perish through my neglect or guilt, will be required at my hands." The prospect of entering the priesthood with so weighty a responsibility had filled him with greater fear than joy.

He lowered his quill into the inkpot—so familiar was this habit that he no longer had to look down to do it. Instead he gazed on the massive heap of stone before him, the Glärnisch Mountain. At its base spread a broad meadow, cut through by the Linth River. A dozen brown and white cows grazed lazily on the lush vegetation, methodically stirring flies off their backs with their long tails. The pastoral scene was reminiscent of his own home and a thousand other places throughout the confederation.

Ulrich's pen scratched across the stiff paper.

"There was a garden spot hedged about on one side by high mountains, on another by gurgling streams, and in it roamed, cropping the green blades of grass, a fat bull of ruddy hue, with widespread horns and on his brow rich-waving hair."

"The bull was happy and safe within his field. By his side panted his faithful dog, who dutifully warned of encroaching predators. Those who would dare attack the bull would be sent flying by his mighty horns. But one day, a cunning creature—a variegated leopard—hatched a plan to seduce the bull into his service by promising him greener pastures. The bull consented—against the protest of his dog. By his trickery, the leopard engaged the bull in all his battles, in which the bull received grievous wounds. Before long, a lion, hearing of the leopard's success, sought to steal the bull to his service. When the bull declined, the lion approached the leopard to form a dangerous new alliance against the bull. When all seemed lost, the herdsman, after much hunting, found the bull and persuaded him to return home, to the great joy of the dog."

A barking dog, just outside the rectory window, momentarily drew together the stares of the grazing cows and the writing priest. When the cows lost interest and returned to grazing, the writer finished.

"By the herdsman I mean the Pope, by the dog the clergy, while by the lion I mean the Holy Roman Emperor, the French king is represented by the leopard, and the common people by the bull."

"Now," sighed Ulrich, "If only my readers will learn the lesson of *The Fable of the Bull* and resist the lure of war and wealth."

Ignoring the counsel of their pastor's first published work, in early 1512 the men of Glarus began to talk openly about marching to Italy to help the Pope drive French out of Milan. Before the late winter chill left the air, citizen-soldiers were on the march. A very interested pastor received detailed reports of the fighting, which he arranged into his second book, *The Italian Campaign of 1512*. Ulrich's heart ached at the thought of his people fighting in a war that had nothing to do with them. At the same time, he was committed to supporting the only church he knew. In deep turmoil, he wrote to his friend Joachim.

"I have greatly missed hearing from you, my dear Joachim, though I know you are always busy with the weightiest of matters. Do not doubt that my affection for you is of such a character that it thirsts for as many letters from you as the Danube has drops of water."

"Everything in Glarus seems uncertain. Every day we receive a letter from the Pope, the Holy Roman Emperor, Milan, Venice, or France—each clamoring about war. Of course, our allegiance is to the Most Blessed Vicar of Christ, Pope Julius. And we are glad that, for now, he has forced the King of France to retreat. We deeply regret that Swiss blood was shed for the victory, nor is it finished flowing."

"Your dearest friend, whose affection pants continually—as with a burning fever—for your reply, Ulrich."

It seemed like just a few days later that Ulrich was startled from his studies by three crisp knocks on his front door. He was not surprised to see the burgomaster of Glarus. Growing up in a politician's house, and being a man of learning, Ulrich had much wisdom to offer the master of the city. What surprised the pastor was the serious and sympathetic look on the mayor's face and the slow pace with which he moved to the chair Ulrich pulled out for him at the table.

"Father," the mayor finally spoke, "Your dislike of foreign fighting is known to all of us." At the word "dislike" Ulrich nearly interrupted. "Hatred" would have been more appropriate.

"For this reason, I regret to inform you that more men from Glarus are marching to Novarra, Italy in a few weeks. I'm telling you this so that you can begin meeting with the families of those men who might not…" The burgomaster turned his face away from the pastor, as he searched for words. "Well, you know the cost of war."

Thoughts of his parishioners dying on the battlefield without their priest offering them last rites flashed through his mind. "So far, I've only heard about the cost of war. I've never yet known it firsthand. I'm going to Italy as chaplain."

The pastor's firm tone of voice convinced the mayor that there was no use arguing.

What the field preacher saw in the Battle of Novarra didn't change his mind about the evil of unnecessary war. But he could not help feeling pride over the prowess of his men. French fighters, numbering roughly 20,000 strong, had laid siege to the city of Novarra. Trapped inside were the armies of the Duke of Milan along with other Swiss mercenaries. On June 6, 1513, 13,000 Swiss soldiers, including fresh reserves from Glarus, swept down on the attackers from all directions in squares ten men wide and ten men deep. The French and their German mercenaries had quickly formed into defensive lines around the city, but they were no match for the relentless Swiss pikemen. Just before the two sides clashed, the Swiss fighters lowered their long pikes to form a deadly wave of spears. The results were decisive. Nearly half of the French army was killed, and the city was liberated.

The thrill of victory momentarily drowned out the cries of those devastated by war.

Three years later, Novarra seemed like a distant memory. Ulrich was back in Italy with his fellow soldiers, most of whom, after two horrendous days of fighting, now lay dead on the smoldering battlefield of Marignano. The pike charge, upon which the Swiss had always depended, was no match for the numerous French cannon. Rapid fire from French guns had made grisly mounds out of the charging Swiss pikemen.

Less than a week earlier, Ulrich had preached to thousands of men with never-dying souls as Swiss troops were preparing for battle. Now, the eternal destiny of many of the soldiers had been forever sealed. Troubling thoughts darted into his mind as he surveyed the devastation. "What was the last thing these men heard from God's messenger? I did my churchly duty; I urged them to rally together as brothers to support our Holy Father's cause, whether just or not. But did I prepare them to meet the Son of God, in whose mouth is a sharp two–edged sword, whose eyes are like a flame of fire, and whose voice is as the sound of many waters?"[1]

Since returning from Marignano, Ulrich's dreams were filled with grisly visions of row upon row of strong

---

1. Cf. Revelation 1:14-16.

and hopeful young Swiss men falling face down, one after another, before French gun fire. On this night, the sound of toppling men grew louder and louder until he awoke in a cold sweat.

To shake his mind from his nightmares, Ulrich lit a candle and retreated to his reading desk. As he turned a crisp new page of Desiderius Erasmus' *Proverbs*, his eyes fell on the first words of a meditation on the horrors of war. "War is approved by the young and inconsiderate, by those who are unacquainted with the dreadful waste of life as well as of property that it occasions."

He read the line over and over. "Exactly!" he said aloud as he underscored the sentence with a thick line from his pen. "Erasmus is right. I must meet this man! Perhaps he can help restore reason to this mad confederacy, and lead us out of the maze of endless warfare."

At the thought of a maze, Ulrich recalled the Greek myth about the labyrinth, which he had read at university. He cleared a space on his desk for a clean sheet of paper and began to retell the old story, now with a new explanation.

"The labyrinth is the worry and work of this world. Theseus, the bold hero, is a man of honor who sacrificially defends his native land. The monster is shame, sin, and vice. The thread by which Theseus retraced his steps out of the maze is intelligence. The maiden, whom Theseus claims at the end, is the reward of virtue."

Ulrich Zwingli

With the needless death of thousands of his countrymen still on his mind, the pastor of Glarus scratched out the conclusion to his poem.

> We go to war, and love to fight.
> We plague our friends and mar the right.
> What can we show for all our ardor?
> Our very lives we lose in barter.
>
> In us God's love does not abide
> Else surely we would turn aside
> From evil and each vain endeavor;
> Our quest for gain and earthly treasure.
>
> We swear that Christian is our name.
> But do we fly that flag in vain?

The last question was directed to greedy warmongers. But even the poem's author had begun to ask the question of himself.

A Step Closer to Zurich

"Master Zwingli, you have a letter!"

The delivery boy ran to catch up with the priest who had just returned from teaching Latin at the grammar school he had started for the boys of Glarus.

"Where is it from?" asked the pastor, kindly, though he neither broke his determined stride nor turned to look back.

"Basel." That one word stopped the priest in his tracks. A hopeful smile broke over his face as he spun on his heels to face the panting lad. The boy handed over the letter and turned to go on his way.

"Stick around, my boy," Ulrich urged. "If the letter says what I hope it does, I'll share my joy with you. If not, I'll need someone to cheer me."

"Erasmus of Rotterdam, now exiled to Basel, to Ulrich Zwingli at Glarus, a philosopher and theologian most learned, and a defender of the faith. The fact that you are so well disposed towards me has been a very great delight as is your letter which was equally animated and educated. I am greatly pleased by your desire to meet me at my "court," as you call it, that we might share, with our other friends, in the joy of learning. Do come swiftly. Farewell from Basel."

"You're a good fellow!" said the pastor, nearly shouting for joy. He dropped a coin in the boy's pocket, gave a few friendly tugs on the lad's cap, and nearly ran the rest of the way to his house.

He was going to visit the most learned man of the day, if not of the entire middle Renaissance age!

"My dear Ulrich ..." said Erasmus, as a servant ushered him into the sitting room. Ulrich was overwhelmed by the seemingly endless rows of beautiful leather books that lined the shelves from floor to ceiling. The rawhide smell of old and new books made him smile. Just a few months earlier, Pope Leo X had bestowed upon his increasingly popular young priest a not-insignificant yearly stipend, which Ulrich was using to stock his growing library. But, as yet, Erasmus' library dwarfed his own.

"It is my distinct honor to welcome you into my humble home. Let me introduce you to two of the most venerable servants of Christ in this entire city." As Erasmus spoke, the two men flanking the scholar blushed. "I'm sure you'll grow to love them as I do. Oswald Myconius—well, I call him Myconius after that most worthy son of Apollo—is the rector of St. Peter's school. Johannes Oecolampadius is the gifted new cathedral preacher. He always 'lights' up the 'house.'"

Ulrich was proud of himself for catching Erasmus' pun on the preacher's Greek last name. He laughed vigorously.

It wasn't long before the conversation turned to Greek, as the study of the old language had become newly fashionable.

"Master Zwingli," began Oswald, "We were just praising Erasmus for his monumental publication of the Greek New Testament. How have you found it?"

"I am but a beginner in Greek, compared to Masters Erasmus and Oecolampadius." Ulrich knew that the two men had worked together on the historic project. "I only began studying the language a few years ago. Or, should I say, God stirred me to the study. Of course, I study Greek not for glory but to unlock the treasure of sacred literature. And, indeed, it has begun to change me and my parish. My preaching in Glarus is no longer a static collection of sayings from the fathers. It is a vibrant stream, flowing from the source of all wisdom."

"Do you think you'll stay in Glarus?" asked Johannes. Ulrich couldn't tell if the question hinted at the possibility that the popular preacher might advance to a more prestigious parish.

"I would like to. And I think the people would like to keep me. They've just begun building me a new rectory. But things are...well, *awkward* in Glarus after Marignano," answered Ulrich.

"Of course they are," replied Erasmus, in a tone that approached sternness. "Despite your opposition to that accursed practice of mercenary fighting, you excessively supported Rome in her conflict with France. Now that Glarus has made peace with France, you've become politically offensive. If I could offer you some personal advice, you need a change of scenery."

No one said what everyone was thinking. Erasmus himself had only recently relocated to Basel to seek reprieve from the flak he faced for criticizing the Roman Catholic Church.

Late into the night, the men talked. Ulrich felt almost intoxicated in the presence of such a learned man as Erasmus. But one thought kept coming back to him: "You need a change of scenery."

Upon his return to Glarus, one of the first things Ulrich did was pen a thank you letter to his hero, complete with the unseemly mountain of praise that was expected among scholars of the day.

"To Erasmus of Rotterdam, great philosopher and theologian, Ulrich Zwingli sends greeting. When I am about to write to you, Dr. Erasmus, best of men, I am on the one hand frightened by the luster of your learning, and on the other hand I am invited by that well known gentleness of yours which you manifested towards me, when I recently came to Basel to see you. It was an unusual proof of kindness that you did not despise a man who is a mere infant, an unknown smatterer. For without boasting you are so much beloved by me that I cannot sleep without first holding conversation with you through your most enlightened writings."

"I was not at all disappointed by the journey I made to see you. In fact, I make my boast in nothing else than this: I have seen Erasmus."

"I also inform you, O father of learning, that, upon your advice, I am relocating—for a time—to Einsiedeln. From there you should expect my next letter of admiration. Your affectionate friend, Ulrich."

* * *

"This is one staring contest I'll never win," thought Ulrich to himself.

The pastor was gazing into the half-closed, unblinking eyes of the famous statue of the Virgin Mary, housed in his new church in Einsiedeln. Ten thousand pilgrims a week came to receive a blessing from the "Black Mary"—her face, as well as the face of her child, was darkened by almost 700 years of candle smoke. Both mother and child were elaborately clothed and wore bejeweled crowns upon their heads.

The crowds would soon throng the image, passing through the abbey gates upon which were inscribed this promise: "Here, a complete remission of sins may be obtained for looking upon the Virgin." The pastor continued to reflect in the pre-dawn, candle-lit church. "Can godliness really come from visiting a dumb image?"

"It isn't helping me!" This time his audible words, nearly a shout, echoed through the empty church.

Ulrich had been reading the Bible like never before. He was beginning to see the need for a living, marriage-like relationship with Christ. But he could not seem to shake the great urge for human intimacy, which would leave him tossing and turning on his empty bed most nights. He was supposed to be married to God, married to the church. But he was burning for close human companionship. Sometimes his desires would overtake him. Last night had been no exception.

"I need to clear my head," thought Ulrich as he leapt from his bed. He quickly got dressed, grabbed his coat, and slammed the door on his empty, lonely house.

Plodding through the quiet hilly streets was refreshing. So was the brisk wind. The pastor tugged the top of his coat closer to his face to keep out the cold.

"I have taken a vow to never marry. But my body doesn't seem to care about that promise! God was right: 'It is not good that man should be alone!'"[1]

Turning a corner, in the narrow, descending street, he saw just what his better nature had been trying to avoid, but which a stronger longing seemed to be steering him toward all along. His desperate eyes glimpsed the mysterious house of ill repute, about which he had sometimes warned his young students. The pastor's feet fastened to the cobblestones. His heart pounded wildly. His conflicting thoughts swirled into a fog.

He turned the other way.

Then he stopped and turned again.

Twice more he retreated and returned.

---

1. Genesis 2:18

Finally, impulsively, against his better judgment which had been growing fainter all along, he hurried down the street toward the heavy, windowless, wooden door. Pressing close to the door to avoid being seen, he prepared to knock. Before his knuckles touched the plank, a disreputable woman opened the door, splashing warm candlelight on the cold street. His pupils dilated. His conscience barely fluttered, beat down now by his failure to resist temptation. Without saying a word, she bid him enter. The door shut behind them with the same hollowness that Ulrich felt in the pit of his stomach.

Early the next morning, with the perfume of the immoral woman still on his face, the pastor thought, prayed, and wept before the silent Virgin Mother's image.

"I need God's power," he cried, growing increasingly frustrated by the heartless gaze of the statue. "I need satisfying food for my soul."

He left the church, feeling disgusted with himself.

As was his habit, he retreated to his standing desk. He opened a leather folder containing dozens of beautifully penned pages. On the last page, the writing stopped in the middle of the first column.

Ever since arriving in Einsiedeln, he had been painstakingly copying Paul's letters, in Greek. Ulrich opened Erasmus' Greek New Testament and began to read the next verse as his hand moved methodically toward the ink well. "... if they cannot exercise self-control, let them marry. For it is better to marry than to burn with passion."[2] He struggled to avoid quivering as he wrote. Inking his pen again, he wrote in the margin, this time in Latin, "For a Christian, there is nothing between chastity and marriage. He must either live chastely or marry a wife."

Around this time, Ulrich began to hear the first whispers about the sudden conversion and growing popularity of a German monk named Martin Luther. Luther had come to see that peoples' sins are forgiven only when they receive Jesus' righteousness by believing the gospel. This same truth had been slowly breaking into Ulrich's heart. Through copying his Greek New Testament, he had already learned that sinners—fornicators included—are washed, sanctified, and justified "in the name of the Lord Jesus and by the Spirit of our God."[3]

Ulrich's preaching began to focus more on the good news about Jesus and less on the rituals the church required. And with a steady stream of people visiting Einsiedeln each week to view the Black Mary, news of this Bible-preaching priest spread.

Near the end of 1518, Ulrich received two letters from people who had noticed his preaching. The first was from Rome, the most important city in Europe; the second from Zurich, the most important city in the confederacy.

---

2. 1 Corinthians 7:9
3. 1 Corinthians 6:9-11

"To our Ulrich Zwingli, beloved in Christ, eternal salvation in the Lord. Our lord, the Pope, watching over you as a father does his children, has noticed your character as a man of letters, and as shining in virtues and merits, and has heard of your laudable reputation. He does, thereby grant you the title and position of papal chaplain along with all attendant honors. So press on from good to better in zeal for virtue, so that in the sight of our lord, the Pope, you shall ever establish yourself as worthier of greater rewards."

"Good grief! If the Pope only knew about my 'shining virtues and merits,'" muttered Ulrich.

The next month, Ulrich received a letter from his new friend, Oswald Myconius.

"My dear Ulrich, I trust you have heard about the opening at the Great Minster Church in Zurich. You know about the prestige of the church; Zurich continues to hear more about you. Though, to be frank, some are making noise about your—I'm not sure what to call them—'moral indiscretions' in Einsiedeln. I sincerely hope this hurdle can be overcome and that you will be pleased to be our next minister."

Ulrich wrote back, "My faithful friend, while I am overjoyed at the possibility of ministering in Zurich, I am grieved that the faults in my character cast a dark shadow over the whole affair. It is true that I have sinned with women. Christ has been blasphemed through me. This fact I hate. Alas, I have fulfilled the proverb: 'A dog returns to his own vomit.'[4] May God, and the people of Zurich, not hold it against me!"

Oswald and other Zurich friends worked to calm the concerns of those who would shortly vote for a new minister.

That same month it was announced: "Ulrich Zwingli will be the next pastor of Zurich's Great Minster Church!"

---

4. Proverbs 26:11.

First Year in Zurich

Ulrich's oxcart lumbered along on the rough road that led to Zurich. It was two days after Christmas, 1518. As raindrops began to speckle the puddles which already dotted the muddy road, Ulrich cast an anxious glance backwards as he lifted the canvas awning that covered the cart's box. "Your precious cargo will be fine," laughed the servant who had been sent from Zurich to help relocate the new Great Minster priest.

"Those books are my dear friends. I'd sooner lose every other earthly possession than my library," replied the pastor.

"Yes, and they are well crated and covered with a greased cloth under the canvas," assured the servant.

Somewhat relieved, Ulrich looked ahead again. As the road bent to the right and descended a small hill, Lake Zurich, which had been occasionally visible through breaks in the fir forest, now lapped the shore immediately to their right. Small sailboats, carrying cargo and fishermen, skimmed the surface of the quiet lake. Straining his eyes, he could sometimes now see the walls of the great city. Rising above the walls, he could see the towers of the two great churches of the city, the Great Minster and the Mary Minster. He could not yet see the massive sandstone statue of armor-clad Charlemagne, wearing his gold crown and holding in both hands his gold-hilted sword. Charlemagne perched imposingly on the wall of the Great Minster, symbolically overlooking the city he had founded and visited.

He thought about the shopkeepers, tailors, brewers, bakers, butchers, cobblers, carpenters, fishermen, and the rest of the roughly 5,000 residents of the city, who would look to him for spiritual guidance.

The servant was startled when his companion blurted out after a moment's silence, "I'm not going to do it, you know."

"Sir?" he questioned.

"The leaders of the church, the canons, will expect me to hire a substitute to do all the preaching so I can focus on gathering in the tithes. But I'm not going to do it. For too long, Christ has been hidden from the people beneath tradition and man-made rules. I've not come to line the church's coffers while some hireling repeats the opinions of the Fathers. I've come to preach the gospel!"

Already the optimistic pastor could envision his parishioners turning from superstition to the living Christ. He imagined the city as it could be, when business owners, politicians, soldiers, and ordinary men, women, and children, bowed beneath the Word of God.

"God can do great things in this city!" exclaimed the pastor.

The servant, surprised by the outburst of emotion, stammered—with considerably less conviction—"I'm sure he can, sir."

On the evening of his thirty-fifth birthday, Ulrich climbed the steps of the Zurich pulpit to preach his first sermon as the newest priest in the city. He was not scared, exactly. Still his left hand trembled slightly as it gripped the rail to steady his climb. He had already informed the canons, in no uncertain terms, that he was called to preach, and his source would be the Word of God alone. He was about to open his mouth as a spokesman for the living God.

The listeners naturally assumed that the priest would read the expected text from the lectionary, or official Bible reading schedule of the church, before offering a few general and historical comments. What they heard instead seemed to be the very voice of God.

After the service, the church courtyard buzzed with excitement. So unusual was Ulrich's style, the people hardly knew what to think. Curious students approached their teacher, Oswald Myconius, to ask his opinion. Flushed with pride, and speaking more loudly than was necessary, Ulrich's old friend answered, "Never have I seen a preacher with such a powerful presence. If I knew it not to be impossible, I would have thought that I had heard an apostle today."

"Master Ulrich, you are an answer to prayer!" Oswald's face glowed with admiration and gratitude as he spoke to his friend. "Even in these first few months, it seems that most of your hearers are listening with true spiritual interest. God *is* blessing your work."

But Ulrich heard in his friend's voice a hint of sobriety, suggesting that his speech had a more particular motive than praise.

"But?" smiled the pastor, raising his eyebrows as he reclined back on his chair.

"It's just that…you're working too hard," replied the teacher. Ulrich raised his hand to object but his friend pressed on. "You stand at your desk from early morning until midnight, with just a few hours of break throughout the day. Even on your breaks, you keep a tight schedule. You hardly even heat your study," said Myconius with a shiver. "It's freezing in here!"

"If I heat my study…" Ulrich hung his head. "My lack of sleep will catch up with me," he finished sheepishly. "I do need to read, write, and study, don't I?"

"Of course, but you are more than a scholar." Again, Ulrich's hand began to rise. Myconius continued with added strength and speed: "And if you keep up this schedule, your work of reform will be as short-lived as yourself."

After a moment of silence over the startling thought of Ulrich's premature death, the two friends argued a little longer. Eventually, Ulrich could tell it was no use.

"Alright, alright, what do you suggest?"

"Pfäfers."

"What?"

"It's perfect," insisted Myconius. "The hot springs at Pfäfers will be good for your body, and the monastery will be good for your mind and soul. And, most importantly, it's just far enough away that you'll hardly be able to hear news of Zurich at all."

Even on a warm July morning, steam simmered from the frothy waters of Ulrich's bath. "Myconius was right, Pfäfers is nearly perfect," he thought. Ulrich felt as if his stress was mingling with the bubbles and mist and slowly dissipating into the light breeze.

"I'm sorry to be the bearer of bad news, Master Ulrich…" The monk's anxious face indicated trouble. "…But, it's the plague. It has reached Zurich."

At the word "plague" a frigid shiver ran down Ulrich's spine, even as he sat in a hot spring bath.

Knowing full well that his words would have no restraining effect on the pastor, the monk warned, "Everyone who can, is fleeing the city. In other places, the plague has struck down up to half the population. You should stay here till it has passed."

"Thank you, brother. I leave after breakfast," answered the priest.

As Ulrich approached Zurich at the hottest point of late summer, already the unmistakable smell of death, and the anxious faces worn by townspeople, confirmed the monk's report beyond all doubt. A few fresh mounds of soil—hastily dug graves—dotted the landscape.

"God forbid that one of those graves is yours, Andrew." Ulrich tried to fight away the thoughts that his youngest brother, whom he had taken into his home, had succumbed to the plague during his absence. He quickened his pace—nearly running now—along the steeply inclining stone alley that led from the Limmat River, behind the Great Minster church, to his new home. With fears battling his hope, he burst through the door. Startled, Andrew nearly dropped the book he was reading.

"Thank God! You're alive!" cried the priest. "And I intend you to stay that way. Please pack your things. You must return to Wildhaus immediately."

"It is good to see you too, brother," laughed Andrew. "Let us both go home and return again as soon as it is safe." Andrew knew that his request would be pointless.

"Andrew, Satan strains hard to snatch his prey into hell. God has called me to strain harder that my dear people would find their life in Christ, even as death knocks at their doors."

Persuaded by his pastor and brother, Andrew returned to Wildhaus to wait out the plague.

The deadly pestilence raged on through the hot summer. The peoples' priest tirelessly preached to the dying and comforted the grieving. So frequently did Ulrich repeat the Requiem, or Mass of the Dead, that he mumbled the words even in his sleep: *"Requiem aeternam dona eis, Domine"* (Grant them eternal rest, O Lord). Was there a single home in Zurich that didn't lose at least one family member?

In late September, the plague entered the parsonage of the Great Minster church. The exhaustion which Ulrich had felt for some days became unbearable. As he sank into bed, far earlier than usual, he began to fear the worst. The symptoms of the deadly plague were all too vivid. Too well did he realize how few plague victims ever recovered. With a trembling hand, he scratched out a few rhymed lines:

> Help me, O Lord, my strength and rock;
> Lo, at the door I hear death's knock.
> Yet, if thy voice in life's mid-day,
> Recalls my soul, then I obey.
> Uplift thine arm, once pierced for me,
> That conquered death, and set me free.
> In faith and hope earth I resign,
> Secure of heaven, for I am thine.

Ulrich's body writhed under the unrelenting swells of heavy fever and chills. Ulcers seemed to burn his stomach, keeping him awake at night. Food seemed to help the ulcers. But the fever had sapped his appetite. Fever and drugs caused his mind to wander aimlessly for hours—or was it days? In moments of clarity he quickly committed his thoughts to paper, not knowing if they would be his last:

My pains increase; haste to console;
For fear and woe seize body and soul.
Death is at hand, my senses fail,
My tongue is dumb; now Christ prevail.

At times, his grasp on the gospel waned as his mind fixed on his sins and unworthiness. Then the Holy Spirit would sweep a wave of assurance over his troubled soul.

Lo! Satan strains to snatch his prey;
I feel his grasp; must I give way?
He harms me not, I fear no loss,
For here I lie beneath thy cross.

A little life seemed to drain from Ulrich's body every day. Before long, the sad news began to circulate through the confederacy: Ulrich Zwingli is dead.

His friends, even entire cities, mourned the loss of the young reformer.

But the rumors were not quite true. Ulrich was greatly weakened in mind and body—for months he had trouble reigning in his wandering thoughts. But he was alive! He wrote to his family to tell them of his recovery. He also finished the poem he had begun on his "deathbed."

My God! My Lord! Healed by thy hand,
Upon the earth once more I stand.
Let sin no more rule over me;
My mouth shall sing alone of thee.

Though now delayed, my hour will come,
Involved, perchance, in deeper gloom.
But, let it come; with joy I'll rise,
And bear my yoke straight to the skies.

It wasn't long before a courier placed a letter from Wildhaus into the hands of the recuperating minister. It was from Andrew.

"A certain incredible tide of joy swept over me, dear brother, on reading your letter, from which I perceive that you are convalescing daily. What more pleasing news could I have than that you are well! If there is anything I can do for you, you must ask. I shall always be prepared to serve you to the best of my ability with hands and feet. And he shall not see Andrew alive who sees him forgetful of you. Farewell again and again, bear with me kindly and ever put me among those who are most fond of you."

Upon hearing the good news that his brother was well and that the plague was subsiding, Andrew returned to Zurich. He tenderly nursed his brother back to health, though health returned reluctantly.

But it was impossible not to notice that as the older brother grew stronger, the younger brother declined. Andrew had contracted the plague. The fight was short. Andrew died on November 19, 1519. As Ulrich knelt at his brother's deathbed, he was overtaken by spasms of grief and mourning. He cried uncontrollably at the loss of his brother, nurse, and friend. For days, he was suddenly and unexpectedly overwhelmed with sorrow.

When his tears dried, he wrote to his best friend, Oswald Myconius, to tell of the death of this "youth of great promise and excellent parts, whom the plague has destroyed."

On the heels of his brother's funeral, Ulrich finished his first year of ministry in Zurich. It had been a year of tear-filled success. More years like this one seemed certain to be just over the horizon.

Of Meat and Marriage

As Ulrich gained strength after his illness, so too did his reformation in Zurich. Following the death of his brother, Christ became to him more precious, more powerful than ever before. He had become persuaded that a person can only change when God's Word takes root in his heart and begins to rearrange his whole life.

The city council, too, began to see the Bible's power. In 1520, the council declared that Zurich's ministers could only preach Scripture, not the positions of the church. This decision opened the floodgates of dramatic change.

"Sausage, anyone?" Christoph Froschauer's words seemed to deepen the hunger of his weary print-shop workers. The workers were sure their boss must be cruelly joking. They were terribly hungry, but Lent had just begun. Under church law it would be several more weeks before they would be allowed to eat meat again.

After noting the cynical responses of his men, Froschauer continued, as he slid his hands up and down the neatly stacked columns of finished books.

"You've been working so hard to finish this edition of St. Paul's Epistles, I've decided to host a little feast in the parlor. Sausage, cheese, and beer for everyone!"

Froschauer was fully expecting the confused looks on the faces of his men. As the sounds of work ceased, the master printer produced a length of smoked sausage from his shirt pocket and took a large bite.

"Why not?" questioned his full mouth, "You've all been listening to Master Zwingli, haven't you? Can anyone tell me where Scripture commands us to avoid meat during Lent?"

No one answered.

"Would God be pleased to see you men, who are now weary from printing his Word, become further weakened by eating only vegetables?"

One man grew bold. "No, he wouldn't!" Others, sharing his opinion, shook their heads.

Froschauer could tell that some of the men were still anxious about breaking, for the first time, one of the most sacred traditions of the church.

"Would it make you feel better to know," he paused, "That Master Zwingli and Master Leo Jud will be joining us for the feast?" The mention of Ulrich and the escalating volume of the speaker's voice had the desired effect.

Cheers echoed around the shop.

"Finish your work, and then bring your appetites to the parlor!"

The guests were pleased to eat their dinner in the presence of the popular minister. But they were surprised that he seemed to avoid the best parts of the meal.

"Eat, Master Zwingli!" encouraged Froschauer. "Does not God say, 'You may eat as much meat as your heart desires.'"[1]

"It's hard to resist the hearty invitation of my own publisher," returned Ulrich. "And yes, God does not deny his people the freedom to eat meat at any time. But in the very letters that your men finished printing tonight, Paul also writes, 'All things are lawful for me, but all things are not helpful.'[2] Perhaps it will be more helpful for me to defend your "high crime," if I am not implicated in it myself." The pastor's eyes darted playfully around the room.

"Mr. Froschauer," he continued, "If you don't sleep through my sermon this Sunday, you'll have no doubt about my position on the matter; and you'll like what you'll hear."

Four days later, the Great Minster church was fuller than usual. News had spread that Froschauer had been brought before the city council, which had fined him a small sum of money for his sausage feast. Froschauer had defended himself, based on the teaching of his minister. Everyone now wondered: Would their Roman Catholic priest defend church tradition or God's Word?

---

1. Deuteronomy 12:20
2. 1 Corinthians 6:12

Perched in his raised wooden pulpit, the pastor looked lovingly at his people and began his sermon.

"Dearly beloved in God, after you have heard so eagerly the gospel and the teachings of the holy apostles, now for the fourth year, you have been greatly fired with the love of God and of your neighbor. You have also begun faithfully to embrace and to take unto yourselves the teachings of the gospel and the liberty which they give, so that after you have tried and tasted the sweetness of the heavenly bread by which man lives, no other food has since been able to please you. It is no secret that some of you have used this Christian liberty to the great offence of the more...*conventional* among us." The preacher paused as murmurs waved through the cathedral.

"What shall we do?" Another pause.

"We shall listen and understand; open the eyes and the ears of the heart, and hear and see what the Spirit of God says to us."

After surveying many appropriate Bible texts, Ulrich gave his answer: "If you will fast, do so; if you do not wish to eat meat, eat it not; but leave Christians a free choice in the matter."

As worshipers began to fan out from the church on their way home, zigzagging through the narrow alleys, they chattered about the sermon. "Does this mean that the Word of God is more powerful than the bishop? Does the church control the Bible, or does the Bible control the church? Has the church stolen our freedom in other ways?"

Ulrich's walk home was short, just across the courtyard of the cathedral. But many of the worshipers couldn't help noticing that, once again, the pastor barely looked at his front door as he strode past.

"He'll be going to Anna Reinhard's house, no doubt," muttered an old woman to her husband.

"And why not," replied the husband, "She's the most beautiful woman in Zurich!"

Just as the old woman's cane struck the man's stomach, he corrected himself with a grunt, "Ugh! The most beautiful woman besides you, my dear."

"Anna, this morning's sermon has me terribly excited! Could you not feel freedom as people realized that it is no sin to eat meat during Lent? For too long the false prophets of the church have led people about like pigs on chains. But the chains are breaking."

"So, you're going to marry me properly, instead of living like we're ashamed of each other?" she replied.

Ulrich sensed that she wasn't joking. His eyes widened, as his smile gently retreated.

Anna continued, "Does the church have a right to keep clergymen from marrying? Does the Scripture forbid it, or only the bishop?"

"You've spoken well, my dear. Marriage will come. But not yet. God's Word is conquering like a mighty army. The church will change. But until it does, we should be cautious not to give unnecessary offence. Clerical marriage would be a scandal."

"Is living in a secret marriage not scandalous?" asked an incredulous Anna.

"Strangely, no," answered the pastor. He replied slowly and in a distant tone, deep in thought. "At least, not by all. The bishops turn a blind eye toward priests who live as if they were married. The church seems to have a buoyant sense that God was right when he said 'It is not good that man should be alone.'[3] Perhaps God's Word will open their eyes and allow priests to marry."

"I must go. I have an idea of holding a secret meeting in Einsiedeln. We will ask the bishop to allow us to marry. And not just us, but all ministers in the diocese. If he does not listen, we will publish the letter so at least the people will know what God says on the matter. You *will be* my lawfully wedded wife!"

Ulrich kissed his "wife," tousled the hair of her son Gerold, born from a previous marriage, and grabbed his papers and rushed out the door.

"Men, I propose that the letter be affectionate toward the bishop, honest about our failures, and straightforward about the Bible's views on marriage." Ulrich sat at the head of a thick wooden table in a dusty room in an unused wing of the Einsiedeln monastery.

"You've got the pen, paper, and ideas. It looks like you're writing the letter!" joked Ulrich's friend Leo Jud.

"I'll write, as long as you listen and share your thoughts as they come," smiled Ulrich.

---

3. Genesis 2:18

"To the Most Reverend Father Hugo, Bishop of Constance…" Ulrich's pen scratched as he spoke.

"He's more rotten than reverend," offered one of the eleven men seated around the table.

"Flattery will get you nowhere, Simon, except with bishops!"

"We are so sure that you are both a most pious lord and a most loving father…" continued Ulrich; his words met with stifled snickers from around the table.

Finally, came the argument and the request: "Influenced by the Word of God, we are persuaded that it is far more desirable if we marry wives, that Christ's little ones may not be offended, than if, with bold brow, we continue rioting in fornication."

"What happened to your flattering words?" questioned Simon.

"The disease must be boldly disclosed to the physician," intoned Ulrich, answering Simon's question, as his pen glided smoothly across the paper.

"We all know the bishop is not going to listen," reminded one of the pastors.

"You're probably right," replied Ulrich, finally looking up from the finished letter. Then he added with a slight smile, "But the people will."

The sound of laughter filled the sparsely decorated wooden hall. Candlelight flickered gaily upon the guests' brightly colored clothing. Heaped plates of roast brisket and potatoes, and casks of apple ale satisfied the many friends and family members of the happy couple. Fifteen-year-old Gerold had returned from his studies in Basel in time for his mother's second wedding.

The bride whispered into the groom's ear, "It took two years, but you finally married me properly, Mr. Zwingli."

"And you've finally landed the halter upon my neck, though it feels like a gentle yoke, Mrs. Zwingli," teased Ulrich. "The Maker of all things willed from the beginning of creation, when he fashioned for Adam from his rib one woman only as a helpmeet, and not a group or crowd of women! I belong to you, and no one else."

A few days after the wedding, Ulrich received a letter from his friend, Martin Bucer. Standing at his desk, Ulrich read the letter aloud to his wife. "When I read that you have become properly married, I was almost beside myself in great satisfaction. For it was the one thing I desired for you. Not only will you no longer be considered by some to be a fornicator…"

Anna, already round with child, winced as she heard the word "fornicator."

"But I am also confident that Christ will use you as a married man fruitfully in the business of his Word."

Anna's contorted lips smoothed into a smile.

Ulrich finished reading the letter: "I triumph in the fact that now you have come up in all things to the apostolic definition."

As a married man, pastoring a church that was increasingly disinterested in keeping human traditions,

Ulrich Zwingli was better fitting the apostolic definition of a pastor. He was also beginning to be less like a Catholic priest, and more like a Christian minister.

The Great Debater

"Brother Faber," the words belonged to the Bishop of Constance, Hugo by name. As he spoke, his left hand distractedly fingered the lowest of the twelve silk-covered red buttons that held together his shoulder-length cape, "I am sending you to Zurich to meet with that guitarist and evangelical flute player."

The bishop's principal deputy smiled broadly at the insulting reference to the increasingly popular, and highly musical, Swiss pastor. Faber didn't yet hate Ulrich; he had been deeply moved upon hearing the false report of Ulrich's death four years earlier. He smiled at the insult because he craved the bishop's approval.

"But you are *not* to debate him," continued Hugo. "The church does not debate with heretics. The church disciplines heretics. And, quite honestly, this is one heretic who knows how to debate. Listen. Learn. And if possible, woo those wandering sheep back to Rome. I would prefer not to have another 'Luther disaster' here in Switzerland."

Faber's response sounded confident, "As you wish, my lord."

Hugo's right hand held the unsealed and unfolded invitation from the Zurich city council; an invitation to a theological debate. "This presumptuous and childish summons does get some things right."

His left forefinger now searched the text. When he found what he was looking for, he scowled and read aloud.

"For a long time, much dissension and disagreement have existed among those preaching the gospel to the common people, some believing that they have truly and completely delivered the gospel message, others reproving them as if they had not done it skillfully and properly. Consequently, the latter call the former errorists, traitors, and even heretics."

The bishop looked up. "Zurich *has* become a city of dissension, disagreement, and heretics; the prodigal city of the diocese. If this keeps up, I will have to answer to Rome."

"Your Grace, I will—as they request—reprove and teach these Lutheran heretics; even if I must do it in the German tongue, as they insist." As Faber finished his sentence, his face twisted as if he had eaten a lemon. All "respectable" church work was conducted in Latin.

"Don't get too excited, my son. This will be no consequential meeting. Only tinkerers and knaves will be present," concluded Hugo.

From the back of the room, Ulrich could see the clerk's gavel pounding on the dais at the front of the hall. But the roar of the 600 participants drowned out its sound. The steam from so many lungs had frosted the window panes, preventing a view of the snow-covered city. Dozens of horses and mules outside the hall stamped at the snow or munched at scattered piles of hay. Many of the canton's 500 poorly educated clergymen had made the trek on foot, being too poor to own a beast of burden.

The pastor looked down at the freshly-printed *Sixty-Seven Articles* of the Christian faith he had written for the debate. "John Hus was burned at the stake for less than this...," he thought to himself. As his searching eyes fell on the delegation from Constance, he continued his thought, "...burned by the men of Constance."

Finally, the gavel did its job and the clamor of voices gave way to the sound of benches being moved, and bodies being seated. The 600 pastors, teachers, nobles, and councilmen gave their attention to the burgomaster.

"Very learned, venerable, noble, steadfast, honorable, wise, ecclesiastical lords and friends. It is not unknown to you that within our city, state, and confederacy, the preaching of Master Zwingli has created discord and strife. Your lords are tired of complaints against Master Zwingli and wish, with your help, to either correct him by the Word of God, or sustain him by the same. We are all here to listen to your complaints against this man. Who will speak first?"

Faber maintained his composure as one head after another turned in the direction of his crimson cap. When even the burgomaster fixed his eyes on Faber, the deputy spoke. "We are not here to debate but to listen to how…the winds blow in Zurich."

Amid the hushed murmur of responses, a loudmouthed student of Ulrich piped up. "The hottest air always blows from Constance!"

Nervous laughter drummed the hall.

The burgomaster was quick to regain order with his gavel. The room fell silent; awkwardly silent for such a large crowd.

Finally, a visitor from the neighboring canton of Berne and one of Ulrich's supporters stood up and, for a few long seconds, dramatically scanned the crowd before speaking, "Where now are the big moguls that boast so loudly and bravely on the streets? Now step forward! Here is the man. You can all boast over your wine, but here no one stirs."

The crowd—mostly sympathetic to Ulrich—was gaining boldness and erupted in laughter.

As the laughter died down, Faber slowly stood. "Dear sirs," declared the vicar, "We are not here to criticize the good pastors of this parish. We are here to listen and to help judge the complaints against the new doctrines as they might arise."

Ulrich was listening to Faber. But he was also being tugged back to the early years of his training in debate. Through his mind glided memories of conquering fellow students in a clash of ideas. He recalled his longing to be that true philosopher, who, said Plato, can win the soul through discourse. Surely, this was his moment! He silently repeated those three words of Aristotle that could mean life or death in a debate: *ethos, pathos, logos.* Assert your credibility, appeal to emotion, apply sound logic.

Feeling the weight of the moment, Ulrich lifted himself from his bench. For a few seconds, his eyelids veiled the august assembly from his mind as he silently prayed, "*Deus det nobis suam pacem*" (May God grant us his peace).

He opened his eyes and spoke. "You know what a revival has taken place among us during these last five years. The decrepit human laws and statutes have finally begun to give way to the gospel of God's blessed Son, which we have preached from his Word. We have declared that all our true happiness, consolation, and good consists, not in our merits, nor in external works, rather alone in Jesus Christ our Savior, to whom the heavenly Father himself gave witness that we should hear him as his beloved Son. For this preaching I am maligned by many as a heretic, a liar, a deceiver, and one disobedient to the Christian Church. Now, if anyone thinks that my sermons or teachings—you have the summary of my doctrine in the *Sixty-Seven*

Shepherd Warrior

Articles—are unchristian or heretical, let them speak in the name of God. Here I am!"

Faber could not resist the invitation. Gradually, against the counsel of the bishop, against his own better judgment, he was drawn into debate with the "heretic" from Zurich. Back and forth Faber— with better manners—and Ulrich —with stronger persuasion—argued over this basic question: Must the faithful follow the practices of the church or might they instead bow only before the Word of God?

As the lunch hour neared, everyone's thoughts began to turn from church councils and Greek grammar to milk, soup, and freshly baked bread. The burgomaster declared a recess. As most of the participants dispersed to local homes or pubs, the council gathered privately to write up a verdict.

Ulrich walked home to spend the hour in prayer.

The afternoon session began with a reading of the council's decision. "Whereas you all have gathered here to learn how to consider the doctrine of Master Ulrich Zwingli, who has been much accused and at whose teaching many have raised discord in this great city and region, and whereas, the accused has challenged his critics to defend their claim that he is a heretic—though no one has been able to do so. Therefore, the city council of Zurich has resolved that Master Zwingli continue as before to proclaim the holy gospel, and the pure holy Scripture, with the Holy Spirit. Furthermore, all priests and preachers in this city and canton shall do likewise and refrain from slander under strict penalty imposed by this council."

Ulrich exited the hall amidst words of congratulations and under the friendly assault of heavy slaps on his shoulders.

"Where were those who wanted to burn us, and had the wood piled at the stake, Master Zwingli?" asked the preacher from the neighboring village of Kappel. "Why did they not show themselves?"

The victorious pastor answered soberly. "We will see them again, friend. In the meantime, they will build the wood pile ever larger and taller. But Almighty God will help us."

The churches in the canton of Zurich, like the one Ulrich pastored, remained Roman Catholic— for a time. The priests continued to offer the Mass, or the sacrament of the Lord's Supper, in which it was believed that the priest offered to the people the physical body and blood of Christ. The priests still heard confessions and offered absolution for sins. The churches still housed relics and statues of Jesus and the saints. Most people did not fail to observe religious holidays like Lent.

Many of the priests no longer believed that these ceremonies could be defended from the Bible. But the common people could not easily let go of life-long traditions. The city council urged that changes in church life should follow changes in the peoples' minds and hearts. The council was optimistic that

Ulrich's Bible teaching would create an appetite for the changes that would eventually come.

After the debate, Ulrich expanded his *Sixty-Seven Articles* into a full-length book. "The church has departed from the simple, spiritual faith of the New Testament," he argued. "It has become entrenched in ceremonies that actually keep people from experiencing the free grace of Jesus Christ offered in the gospel."

Though the Zurich debate was intended to promote peace, the wave of unrest between traditional Catholics and the reformers continued to swell. Much of the tension had to do with the use of images in worship. In the debate, Ulrich had urged his followers to put their trust in Christ alone and not in the saints. "For I know, and truly find in the divine Scriptures, that Jesus Christ alone can bless us," he had said.

But for centuries the people had believed that they could be helped by praying to the saints. The people had also come to believe that they were helped by paintings or statues of the saints to whom they prayed. Images of Jesus and his more famous followers filled the churches and homes of Zurich. Ulrich was confident that the images could be removed peaceably, perhaps even by the churches. He had written earlier to Bishop Hugo, "When Julius Caesar felt the mortal wound, he folded his garments around him that he might fall with dignity. The downfall of your ceremonies is at hand! See at least that they fall decently, and that light be everywhere promptly substituted for darkness. Help us reform!"

But the downfall of the Catholic ceremonies and the disposing of images was happening too slowly in some people's minds.

A young man named Claude bristled every time he passed by the large wooden crucifix which stood proudly on the property of the town's miller.

"How can people continue to pay respect to that carved tree when the living Christ is always with us in Word and Spirit?" As the thought tumbled around his head, he imagined himself as a modern Gideon who had cut down the Asherah pole in the days of the Midianite oppression,[1] or the missionary Boniface, who had cut down Thor's Oak in eighth century Germany.

On a cool September night, Claude and a group of zealous friends entered the miller's property. Claude gave a brief, invigorating speech about the unlawfulness of graven images. "God would have us taught by his living Word" he declared, raising his shovel handle over his head, "not by dumb images!" At the last word, his spade struck the earth. Within minutes the energetic youths had undermined the image and toppled it to the ground.

Word of the demolition spread swiftly. Claude and his friends were thrown into jail. Venomous words were spoken on both sides of the conflict.

---

1. Judges 6:25-28

"Let those Pontius Pilates be executed!" demanded some. "They have assaulted our Lord!"

"They are heroes!" announced others, "They have put the ax to the tree of superstition!"

"For my sake," Ulrich joked with his friends, "they could leave the idols hanging on the walls and erected on street corners. My eyesight is so bad I can hardly see them at all!"

But when asked by the city council, his answer was balanced. "They have committed no religious crime, though they have broken the law of private property and should be disciplined accordingly. But this kind of thing will continue happening until people better understand the uselessness of religious icons. We need another debate!"

Nearly 900 men packed the town hall in late October 1523. In this debate, Ulrich, Leo Jud, and the other reformed ministers easily proved that the religious use of images had no support from the Bible. The debate also showed that in the Lord's Supper, which was still called the Mass, Christ is neither sacrificed nor do the faithful eat and drink his physical body and blood. Instead, in the Supper, believers request and receive grace and forgiveness by committing themselves to Christ and his finished work.

Over the course of the next year, the old traditions swiftly crumbled in Zurich. The city council ordered the removal of images, relics, and other ornaments. Painters covered over with whitewash the beautiful frescoes on the walls of the churches—the old books for the unlearned. Pastors simplified the ceremonies of worship. The people gradually placed less and less emphasis on saints' days.

The religion of Zurich, Switzerland was changing. Far too rapidly for some. Not nearly quickly enough for others.

New Radicals

"The hand straps are tight, my lord."

Ulrich, lying on his back, tilted his head backward till he could see the straps which linked each of his outstretched arms to the harness of a team of horses. Beside each horse, glowing in the cloud-splotched moonlight, stood a red-clad bishop.

"The feet straps are tight, my lord."

This time the shout came from the direction of his feet. Ulrich jerked his head forward to see straps trailing from his ankles to another team of horses. Beside these horses stood two of his former students.

Sweat poured from the pastor's brow. His heart beat wildly. His breaths came in convulsive gasps.

"Pull!" The shout seemed to come from somewhere below, perhaps from hell.

Ulrich's body tightened as he tried in vain to wriggle free from the two teams of horses that were tearing him apart. His scream pierced the dark night.

"Darling, wake up!" shouted Anna, desperately shaking her husband's shoulders. "You're having a nightmare."

"It was so real!" he blurted, after catching his breath. "And so true. They're pulling me apart from both ends!"

"What do you mean, dear?" Anna asked. Alarm was etched in her face.

"Rome wants to pull off my arms to keep me from meddling with their idolatrous religion. And my own former students—the ones who used to hang on my every word—they want to pull off my legs. They think the reformation is running far too slowly."

It was true. Ulrich had vented about the discouragement that mingled with his joy, following the second Zurich debate. The reformers had soundly defeated the Roman position on the Mass and images, only to be attacked by their own students for not recklessly bringing about the changes they all hoped for. Since that second debate, rumors circulated that the more radical-minded reformers were attempting to start their own churches without ordained ministers or the blessing of the city council.

Still clammy from his nightmare, Ulrich propped himself up in a sitting position against his headboard. Through their bedroom window, the imposing twin towers of the Great Minster pierced the fog in the dimly moonlit sky. "God has brought two siege towers against us, my dear. Will the church build up her walls before one of the towers smashes this little work that God has begun? I expected a fight from Rome, but not from my own friends. Some of these radicals are like sons. Now they've gone to war against me."

Anna pulled herself up close to her husband and lay her head on his shoulder. "They are just impatient and ambitious youths. They want the world to change, just like you do. You were once impatient like them, remember?" Anna blushed. Ulrich turned his head away slightly as he caught Anna's veiled reference to his youthful unchastity. "Perhaps they will listen to the reason of an old... I mean, experienced man like yourself." Anna gently kissed her husband on the cheek and slid back down under the covers. "Just talk with them."

Anna rolled over and pretended to sleep. She smiled slightly when, in a moment, the exhausted pastor's snores droned through the room. But she couldn't sleep.

It was no wonder that her husband dreamt of being martyred. He could no longer go out in the streets alone at night. The Catholic Church wanted him for heresy. Even his hero, Erasmus, had written his final letter to Ulrich, a crushing, disapproving letter of warning. Already, several kidnapping plots had been discovered. The most famous man of Zurich had to take care where he ate and drank, lest he be poisoned. During the winter following the second debate, the citizens of the nearby canton of Luzern had crafted a life-size figure of Ulrich and hung "him" from the gallows. Is this what would become of the real Ulrich?

Anna's trembling fingers smoothed the wrinkles in her pleated brow. She breathed in deeply through her nose. Her exhaled breath fluttered the wisps of hair that hung over her face, which she held in her hands. Silently, she repeated the words of a favorite family Psalm, words King David had penned when his own son revolted against him:

> O Lord, how many they
> Who deeply trouble me;
> How greatly are they multiplied
> Who do me injury.
>
> There is no help for him,
> No help in God, they say;
> Thou art my shield and glory, Lord,
> Thou art my certain stay.
>
> I called to God, He heard
> From out His holy hill.
> I fell asleep, I woke in peace,
> For He sustained me still.[1]

Before she had finished the Psalm, husband and wife were snoring together.

The next evening, as the sun's last light melted into the outline of the city, the Zwinglis' front door resonated with several quick thuds.

"That will be Jud and Myconius," said the pastor, in a monotone, barely looking up from the book spread before him at his standing desk. Finishing the page he was reading, Ulrich quickly slid the book into his bag

---

1. From the metrical version of Psalm 3.

and grabbed his course, heavy, coat which always hung next to his desk. By this time, Anna and the two guests were chatting politely at the door.

"God, be my sword," he prayed, "so I can leave mine sleeping in its sheath." Ulrich's heavy sword slapped against his thigh as he retightened his belt. He no longer left the house unarmed, and never alone at night.

As the three men made their way through the dimly lit city, they conversed in hushed tones.

"If they do not relent, this will be my last private meeting with these rebaptizers," announced Ulrich. "They will sink our ship if they keep flailing about so recklessly. We must win them over or else turn against them what power God has given us."

The others were silent. Their silence seemed to indicate that the one had spoken the thoughts of the three.

"Well, the house looks cheery from the outside," smiled Myconius as the friends approached the well-lit home. "Perhaps we'll find it as happy inside."

Whatever hope Myconius' words might have raised, the opening of the front door threatened to dash. As soon as the host, Felix Manz, escorted them in, a loud voice boomed from the candle-lit table. "You see only three faces, brothers. But, don't be fooled. Six have just entered the house!"

Other men seated on benches lining the table grunted in affirmation of the speaker.

"Which face will you show tonight, masters? The one that shouts for reform or the one that whimpers for peace?"

The speaker, Conrad Grebel, stood up as the guests approached the table. His hands were firmly at his side, his right rested on the hilt of his sword.

Ulrich and his friends calmly took their places at the table.

"Let me say it for the hundredth time." The pastor's voice was calm but firm. As he spoke he looked, one at a time, into the faces of former students, men who had been converted under his ministry, and who used to gather in excited meetings to study notes from his sermons. "I beseech you by Jesus Christ, by our common faith, that you not make any change rashly, but show to all men by your endurance, if in no other way, that you are Christians, in that on account of the weak, you bear things that by Christ's law you do not need to bear."

"Or is it, sir, that you care more for your churchy reputation than for the Word of God? questioned Grebel. "God has spoken. The wicked traditions of Rome cannot be supported by Scripture. Where in the Bible do you find the Mass, infant baptism, fancy priestly clothing? How can you remain Catholic and call yourself Christian?"

Grebel's supporters voiced their agreement.

"You know I agree with you on many points," pleaded the pastor. "For God's sake, you learned most of what you know from me! In time, all of this *will* change, though I have become more than satisfied that the church is not wrong in baptizing the infant children of believers."

"It's always 'in time' with you, Zwingli," snapped Manz. "But the time never comes!"

"Open your eyes, man!" bellowed Ulrich, as he slapped his hands flat on the table. "Things are changing. But Rome wasn't built in a day. Nor will the Roman Church change in a day, perhaps not even in our day."

"Surely not, if we keep following you," someone sneered.

"Then follow Christ," urged Ulrich. "Remember that he was raising up twelve timid men to be the new leaders of the church. He preached and he taught. He answered their foolish questions. He loved them though they were weak of faith. But he was patient. Do you not remember his tender words in John's Gospel? 'I still have many things to say to you, but you cannot bear them now.'[2] And so he entrusted their full understanding to the timely ministry of the Holy Spirit. Follow Christ. Do not despise the day of small things.[3] Right now, the storm cloud of change might be as small as a man's hand. But in time, it will become black and heavy with refreshing rain."[4]

Ulrich brought his speech to a close with three piercing questions: "Will you honor God by submitting to the right leadership of our city council, even as it works to promote the kingdom of Christ? Will you

---

2. John 16:12

3. Zechariah 4:10

4. 1 Kings 18:44-45

stop teaching that young children of believers are not church members? Will you be for us or against us?"

It was a moment of decision.

"We too can quote Scripture," said Grebel. "And we say, 'can two walk together, unless they are agreed?'"[5] With these words he stood and, after locking eyes with his former friend, swept his face toward the door.

Blood throbbed madly into Ulrich's face. His racing mind blocked out all the sound in the room. The flickering, sputtering, candle before him seemed to be mocking everything he was fighting for. The flame danced precariously near the end of the wick. It doubled over, almost out of sight, before offering one last flash. Smoke puffed from the end of the wick. Soon the smoke disappeared. It was gone; the candle, and the once so-promising hope of a unified reform work in Zurich. Dazed, Ulrich closed his eyes and left the house.

The first light of the next morning filtered through the frost-sparkled windows. Already several spent candle stumps littered Ulrich's writing desk. The title sheet before him bore taunting words: *On Those Who Cause Unrest*. The author's heart churned with conflicting emotions. Hatred for the way the young, radical reformers went about trying to topple Rome. Love for their zeal. Old reminiscences of the way his former students had spurred his own courage and imagination that change was possible.

---

5. Amos 3:3

He gritted his teeth and wrote on.

"Some among us are not reformers but revolutionaries who will unravel every fabric of society if they flourish. The apostle John spoke well of them: 'They went out from us, but they were not of us; for if they had been of us, they would have continued with us.'"[6]

Ulrich's new enemies were often called Anabaptists because of their view that those baptized in infancy were not properly baptized. In their estimation, only the baptism of professing believers could be considered valid. Many of the Anabaptists also taught against the system of church tithes, military service by Christians, and the taking of oaths. Their opponents feared that Anabaptist practice would lead to a total breakdown of church and state.

Because baptism was the distinguishing mark of those who could be considered Christian, this issue was hotly contested. In August 1524, the city council made infant baptism mandatory throughout the Zurich canton. In defiance of the law, Grebel and others began rebaptizing church members during the winter of 1525.

Their message was clear. There would not be one reformation in Zurich, but two, with different goals, different temperaments, and different results.

---

6. 1 John 2:19

The End of the Mass

There was no doubt: the church in Zurich, Switzerland, was changing. And as it changed, it began to look increasingly less Roman Catholic. But one thing had not changed. This one thing continued to unite the Zurich churches to the Church of Rome. The reforming churches still practiced the Mass.

In the Catholic Mass, the bread and wine of Holy Communion are believed to mystically become the body and blood of Jesus Christ. With this understanding, Christ is bodily present on the altar. His crucifixion is re-presented before the people. And the worshipers feed on Christ through the mediation of the priest.

It had been twelve years since Ulrich had sat in the Milan Cathedral while serving as chaplain during the Italian Wars. Still, he could clearly recall the wonder that swept over his mind as he learned that a fourth century bishop named Ambrose had made significant changes to the church calendar and the Mass within his parish. Over the years he had often asked himself, "If Bishop Ambrose was able to make changes to the

Mass in his day, is there any reason we can't do the same today?"

For years, Ulrich and his friends—including Leo Jud and Oswald Myconius—had been teaching against the Catholic Mass. So effective had been their teaching that in many parishes Holy Communion was no longer being celebrated at all. The priests were unwilling to read the traditional Mass, but had nothing to use in its place.

On Tuesday afternoon, the week before Easter 1525, Ulrich, Jud, Myconius, and several other ministers sat around the Zwingli table. A small fire crackled on the stone hearth. The men used thick slices of bread to wipe from the bowls the last remnants of potato-cheese soup.

Ulrich slid his fingers under his black wool hat to scratch through his thick red hair. He pondered the words of a minister seated across the table. "Men, if the city council grants this request," the man had said, "we all become heretics. Rome will no longer acknowledge us as Christians or protect us as citizens of God's kingdom."

For a moment, besides the fire, the only sound in the house came from the rocking of Anna's chair in the adjacent parlor as she nursed to sleep the Zwinglis' infant Regula.

"My dear friend," sighed the yes, forty-one year old Ulrich, "that day will soon dawn on us, regardless of this petition. But I say the time is right. We cannot continue to preach a living Christ and then imagine that we can serve him on a platter. The Mass is not a sacrifice, but a remembrance of the sacrifice and assurance of the salvation which Christ has given us. How could our Lord have said, 'Do this in remembrance of me'[1] if in the Supper he would be physically present? One does not 'remember' one whose body is before his eyes. Until our people understand this, they will remain chained to the devices of Rome and her mercenary priests."

While Ulrich spoke, his hands had held open his pocket Bible to 1 Corinthians 11. As both hands formed fists and came to rest firmly on the table, the pages of his Bible fanned shut. The pages stopped at the back paper, on which he had neatly penned dates and events that were close to his heart. The most recent entry read, "Regula Zwingli was born in the year of our Lord 1524, on the last day of July, a Sunday, before daybreak, almost exactly midway between two and three o'clock." The couples' firstborn was named after one of the patron saints of Zurich.

The thudding of her father's fists on the table briefly awoke the nursing baby.

"The people are ready, friends," assured Myconius, after a moment's thought. "And so is the council. Well over half of the great council supports Master Zwingli. And most of them are ready to act."

"If God has so judged," grinned Jud, "Then let's not keep your darling baby awake any longer." He jumped

---

1. 1 Corinthians 11:24-25.

to his feet, swiping the freshly-inked parchment from the table. "Dearest Anna," Jud leaned his head around the wall to look into the parlor; a smile played on his face. "Before this week is up, your husband will be more famous in this diocese than the bishop,"

"Master Jud," she answered, "All I care about is that he is precious in God's eyes. And *that*, he already is."

"And in yours too, I hope?" asked her husband.

"Of course, dear. I wouldn't tolerate all these clandestine meetings in my house if you weren't my most beloved friend."

"She's an angel of a wife, men!" Ulrich said with more than usual passion.

"Let's be going, brothers, before our 'Eros' gets sidetracked," joked Jud.

"And be going with courage, men," added Ulrich. "As you take your well-filled stomachs with you, take also God's Word. It is the Word of God that sustains the soul of man, as food sustains his body."

As the pastors approached the thick paneled doors of the city hall, they were joined by burgomaster Roust, who with the cuff of his jerkin was just wiping off from his mustache the last of his grilled fish. "Judging by the determined looks on the faces of this fine assembly, I think I should return to the pub for another drink," muttered the burgomaster. "Your business smells of trouble, or I'm not the master of this city," he finished.

"Lord Roust," answered Ulrich, "The only trouble we hope to create, is for those taskmasters who hold the children of your dear city in spiritual prison. We aim to break their necks and we think you and your friends will help."

They did. By a narrow vote, the council ruled that in Zurich, the Catholic Mass would be replaced by a simple, biblical communion service. In two days' time, the reforming churches of Zurich would make their most daring and definitive break from the old Roman Church the people had always known.

The waning sun flicked the colors of stained glass upon the worshipers as they entered the Great Minster church. By custom, the men and women separated at the aisle and sat on opposite sides. It was Maundy Thursday, the day to remember when Christ washed the feet of his disciples and served them their Last Supper together. A rumor had spread that the Mass had been outlawed in Zurich. Out of habit, and now also out of curiosity, the worshipers glanced in the direction of the altar, the table upon which the priests had always claimed to re-present Christ's sacrifice on the cross and from which they claimed to distribute the real body and blood of Jesus. What they saw was unrecognizable. It seemed that all eyes were fastened on the strange sight at the front of the church.

Gone was the massive stone table, wrapped with an ornamental stole, and covered with a red silk canopy which—suspended above the table—had protected the altar from dust. Gone were the ornate brass candlesticks, old symbols of the two peoples, Jews and Gentiles, who rejoiced at Christ's birth. Gone was the cross, which had always stood between the two candlesticks. Gone was the chalice, the gold wine goblet, lavishly adorned with precious stones, and the matching gold box that housed the bread. Gone was the sun-shaped shrine into which a piece of bread was placed to be displayed to the faithful.

Instead, they saw an ordinary wooden table, draped with a clean linen cloth. Upon the table sat wooden plates of bread and wooden cups of wine. More than one worshiper—of the more educated sort— remembered that wooden vessels could not be consecrated by the bishop. What they were about to celebrate would not be a Roman Catholic Mass.

When Catholic priests performed the Mass, they stood between the congregation and the altar, with their backs to the people. But after leading the people in prayer and Scripture readings, and delivering a brief sermon, Pastor Zwingli—wearing his dark scholar's gown—descended the pulpit and stood behind the table facing the congregation. His face was sober, but welcoming. His bright eyes spread among his friends the love he had for them in his heart.

He opened his Bible to the sixth chapter of John's Gospel. The people expected him to begin reading in Latin, the language of scholars and of the church. But the words that they heard next made sense. They were German words. The same words with which mothers soothed their disconsolate children. The same words with which a man encouraged his friend.

"Listen to the words of our beloved Savior," began the minister. "Most assuredly, I say to you, he who believes in Me has everlasting life. I am the bread of life... I am the living bread which came down from heaven. If anyone eats of this bread, he will live forever; and the bread that I shall give is My flesh, which I shall give for the life of the world."[2]

"You hunger and thirst. But not just for food. In this meal you receive food and drink but not through your mouths. You who take part in this public thanksgiving prove to the whole church that you are of the number of those who trust in the Christ who died for us. Believe in Christ and be thankful!"

With warm solemnity Ulrich passed the wooden plates to his attendants, who passed them down the pews of Christian worshipers. As each plate was passed, a neighbor or family member held it out to their friend, who tore off a piece of bread with their own hand. With wide eyes and pounding hearts, the worshipers also received the wooden cups of wine—for centuries the average churchgoer was denied the cup. Each worshiper took an invigorating swig of wine before passing the cup to their brother or sister. For the first time, the congregation of the Great Minster experienced a family

---

2. John 6:47-51

meal, commemorating the suffering and death of their Lord. No longer was a priest mediating their religious experience. Instead, brothers and sisters passed between themselves a memorial of the reconciling work of Jesus.

At the conclusion of the meal, the congregation stood to raise their voices with the words of Psalm 113:

> He lifts the poor and makes them great,
> With joy He fills the desolate;
> Praise ye the Lord and bless His name,
> His mercy and His might proclaim.[3]

The reformed church in Zurich had formally severed ties with Rome. The poor and desolate people of the canton had never felt so great or joyful.

---

3. From the metrical version of Psalm 113.

War of Water and Words

Long after most of the lights had been extinguished in the homes of Zurich, two unstable figures rambled out of the pub that squatted in the shadows of the Great Minster on the edge of the Limmat River. They were on a mission, though their wobbly legs showed that they had sat too long carping around a pitcher of ale that night.

Their slurred conversation in the pub, sometimes rising to a fevered pitch, always seemed to return to the Zurich reformation. The men were too impious to appreciate the reformation of religion that had been gaining momentum in the canton. But they had strong feelings about the reformation of morals. Under Ulrich's influence, sexual immorality was no longer tolerated. The church now had the authority and will to excommunicate—or put out of the church—unchaste church members.

"As I see it, he ain't got no business directing my private carryings on," grumbled one of the men. "Soon they'll criminalize swearing, dice, and cards!"

"Agreed," added his friend, after taking a long swig of beer. "The old way was better. The private confession and a few pence in the plate was a small fee for living how we pleased."

"If Zwingli wants to live holy, let him," suggested the first speaker. "But let him stay out of our business."

As the men growled and drank, the conversation turned violent.

"Let's see how he likes it to have someone meddle in *his* sleeping chamber!" snarled one of the men.

"Not so loud, you oaf!" cautioned his friend. "Who knows who's listening these days?"

With the stealth of tumbling boulders, the two men lumbered out the door toward the Zwinglis' house. Wheezing and tottering from the uphill walk, the drunk men each drew a heavy cobblestone from the folds of their shirts. Their unsteady throwing arms waved back and forth a few times before sending the projectiles toward the small window, just a few feet out of their reach.

The first stone thudded into the stucco wall and fell to the ground. The second shattered the window and disappeared into the room.

Shards of glass and splinters of wood sprayed across the Zwinglis' bedroom.

"Ulrich!" screamed Anna, pulling the covers over her and Regula. The one-year-old baby, jostled awake, added her screams to the commotion.

Ulrich had already grabbed his sword and was dashing toward the front door.

"If you have any business with me," he shouted, "Come back tomorrow morning at daylight! We can settle the business like men and not like nocturnal cowards!"

The drunk vandals had already bumbled around a corner into the thick night shadows.

By the time Ulrich had returned to the bedroom, Anna had quieted the baby and was sweeping up the debris. Her husband bent down to pick up the rock that had rolled under the bed. As his knees touched the ground, he grabbed his stomach, unsuccessfully suppressing a groan.

"You're having those spasms again, aren't you, dear?" asked Anna, pained by her husband's distress. "Will you please see a doctor in the morning?"

Ulrich knew that his wife's gentle tone would escalate in strength if he resisted. "I will...but only after I consult with Joachim first."

Since the two friends had been in college together in Vienna, Joachim Vadian had graduated as a doctor of medicine after studying under the personal physician of the Emperor Maximilian I. For the last several years Vadian had served as the city doctor in a nearby canton.

Having lost all hope of sleep, Ulrich retreated to his standing desk to pen a letter to his old friend.

"My dear Vadian, it was a strange day yesterday. As usual, I began the day by preaching at the Great Minster's six o'clock service. By eight, I was lecturing from the book of Exodus in our brand new theological school, the Carolinum. You'll see why Exodus was suitable after you hear what 'plagues' me. Having gone for my bath at nine o'clock and had myself bled, I nearly fainted on the way home. By the end of an hour, I was more or less myself again, but only managed with difficulty to suppress the groaning which came from a weak heart. At two o'clock in the afternoon, I was overcome by sleepiness—but as soon as I awoke, I was the old Zwingli again! Good thing too. Because a 'little bird' flew through our window last night and kept us awake. While cleaning up, I accidentally allowed my wife to notice the sharp pain in my stomach."

"I always remember your former medical instruction; you told me that, once a month, I ought to relieve my liverishness by taking preserve of roses. Still, I'm afraid, the pains are becoming more frequent. As always, I await your good counsel, trusting that your prescription will include a hearty dose of music on the lute!"

"Give our love to your bride. And do persuade her that we have done our best to counsel her mischievous brother—Conrad Grebel—to leave his revolution and patiently work for reform. But it seems that he craves a complete overthrow of the old faith. May God bring him back to his senses!"

Life in Zurich was stressful enough on a good night's sleep.

As the tired and pained minister made his way to the city clerk, who would dispatch his letter to Vadian, he debated just what he would say at the council meeting, which was about to commence. Ulrich had been quarreling with the council over a public challenge issued by Rome to again debate the theses of the reformation. He had already accepted the challenge of the celebrated Catholic debater, Johann Eck. But Eck would not agree to come to Zurich. And the council would not allow Ulrich to travel to a Catholic canton.

"We are having a hard enough time keeping you safe in our own city," declared the burgomaster. "The carpenter tells us that it was not, in fact, a bird that broke your window last night. Stones like that will smash your bones, not your window, if you fall into the wrong hands. You are not leaving this city with our blessing—or promise of protection—unless it is to another city friendly to our cause."

"Besides," argued another councilman, "No Protestant can win this debate. Rest assured, this Baden Conference will be a Roman Catholic gala. We will be terribly outnumbered and the rules—and voters—will all favor Eck. We will keep you alive for a fight you can actually win."

The councilman was right. Despite sound debating by good men including Johannes Oecolampadius, the national judges, speaking on behalf of the whole Swiss confederacy, affirmed traditional Catholic teaching in May 1526.

Rome, supported by nearly the entire confederacy, was trying hard to choke out the reformation from the outside. Meanwhile, the teaching of the radical reformers, the Anabaptists, threatened to ruin the movement from within. The city council believed that the reformation could not succeed with the constant in-fighting instigated by the radicals.

A few months after the Baden Conference, the city council enacted a terrible law that threatened with drowning those who were convicted of rebaptizing. Fueled by zeal for the reformation, Ulrich wrote a little book in which he laid out a biblical, practical, and historical case in favor of baptizing the children of believers. "The children of the Hebrews, because they, with their parents were under the covenant, merited the sign of the covenant. In the same way, Christians' infants, because they are counted within the church and people of Christ, ought in no way to be deprived of baptism, the sign of the covenant." Sadly, much of this book was filled with extremely harsh language against the Anabaptists. He called them "apostles of the devil," "atheists," and "most seditious men." If this were not enough, he suggested that "the case of these people is worse than my pen can show."

This was the situation in Zurich on an early January day in 1527, when Felix Manz ignored his oath to never return to the city and to never rebaptize those whom the church had already baptized. The council had thrown him in prison.

During the lunch hour, rumors spread that Manz would be executed that day. "He who dips will be dipped" was the enthusiastic anthem of many Zurich citizens as they gossiped about Manz's crime. Crowds of friends, family members, and curious citizens gathered along the snow-dusted streets around the Wellenburg prison tower as the burgomaster, several council members, clergy, and constables began to enter the gates. As Manz emerged, his mother let out a painful shriek before cupping her hand over her mouth to muffle the cries. The prisoner was led toward the fish market along the Limmat River.

The mingled voices of the crowd hushed as Burgomaster Roust read the sentence. "Felix Manz shall forthwith be punished with drowning for troubling this city with doctrines that contradict the Word of God and the law of this city."

"He who dips will be dipped!" shouted a few irreverent voices.

Snow crunched under the weight of constables as they walked the bridge that spanned the frigid Limmat. The boat that was tied to the bridge bobbed into the water as the constables lowered themselves and Manz into the craft. From the shore, the audience could hear Manz preaching and praying. A reformed minister also entered the boat, urging the prisoner to change his mind before it was too late.

"Be strong, son! Trust in God!" wailed his mother.

As the boat floated down the river, the constables bound Manz' hands and pulled them behind his knees, sliding a pole between them. At 3 o'clock, he was pushed from the boat into the freezing water. Those on shore could hear his last words: "Into thy hands, O God, I commend my spirit."

The shouts of "he who dips will be dipped" seemed to have been silenced with Manz. Surely there were better ways of promoting the truth.[1]

An opportunity to pursue a better way presented itself the next year. The reformation had been growing in the nearby canton of Berne.

"Help us decide to which faith we should hold," the Berne city council wrote to Zurich.

Zurich's council deliberated on the request and on Ulrich's desire to participate. "We will send you," they decided, "but only under heavy guard."

On the first day of 1528, nearly 100 of the most important Zurich citizens, including Burgomaster Roust and Ulrich, began the trip to Berne under the care of 300 soldiers. Their entrance into the friendly city resembled a festive parade. Before the start of the conference, Ulrich spent precious time with Vadian, Oecolampadius, and other old friends. He also made many new friends, including a young man named Heinrich Bullinger. "How refreshing," he thought, "to be among men of like passions and convictions!"

During the conference Ulrich sat at a table scattered with books, papers, ink, and quills. Onto this table someone quietly placed a folded sheet of paper with Ulrich's name written on the outside. The paper

---

1. See appendix on "The Use of Religious Force during the Reformation."

fluttered in his unsteady fingers. He could not forget the note he had received from Anna a few days earlier. In that letter she had lamented that her daughter Margaret, from her previous marriage, had just lost her first child. Anna herself was about to give birth again. Ulrich's heart leapt out to his wife and their child in her womb.

With trembling hand, he slid the paper to the center of his desk and opened the fold.

"Congratulations, you have another child!"

At once, the speaker at the front of the hall seemed to fade into the distance as Ulrich began scribbling a letter to Anna. "Grace and peace from God! Dearest wife, I thank God that he has bestowed on you a happy birth. May he help us to bring up the children according to God's will. Send to my cousin one or two hats of the same style and quality as those you wear. She has been beyond measure kind to me and to us all and deserves to look as pretty as you! Herewith I commend you to God! Pray for me and for all of us. Give my love to all your children, especially Margaret; comfort her on my behalf. Ulrich Zwingli, your husband. P.S. Send me the dirty old overcoat as soon as you can. It's a bit cold being so far away from you!"

Near the end of his time in Berne, Ulrich was given several opportunities to preach. On one occasion, as he ascended the raised pulpit, a Catholic priest also approached the stone altar to say Mass. Perhaps out of curiosity, the priest waited to first hear Ulrich's sermon,which included a thorough critique of the Mass. At the close of the sermon, the priest shed his ornate robe and placed it on the table. Those seated nearby heard him mutter. "If that's what the Mass is, I'll never hold one again."

But for every Catholic priest who came to agree with the reformation, many more were helping to fan into flames a growing hatred of the new movement.

The First Kappel War

"We need facts, gentlemen!" Urgency spilled from Burgomaster Roust's mouth.

A dozen grim faces, belonging to councilmen, military generals, and one famous pastor—all pale from a dark and stressful winter—met his stare. The table before them was scattered with maps, letters, and wooden plates piled high with cheese wedges and sausage links. Directly behind the burgomaster, hung Zurich's coat of arms: a shield with one half painted white, the other blue. The blood-red banner flying from the shield was an undying reminder of an ancient defeat in battle.

This was a council of war.

"The fact is, Master Roust," answered Ulrich, "that the smoke of Jacob Kaiser's burnt body is right now repulsing the nostrils of God. How many reformed ministers will be sacrificed on the pyres before we act? The Lutherans and the Catholics—both of whom think we've reformed too much —would see our 'sect' exterminated. And they are mounting the means by which to do it."

The leading men of the city observed an unbidden moment of silence for the deceased minister. Just a few days earlier, Kaiser had been kidnapped by Catholic henchmen as he was traveling to the church at which he had just been appointed pastor. The Zurich council had petitioned Schwyz, a Catholic canton, to release him at once. "If you harm the good minister of our state, you will be blasting a war trumpet which we will answer with full force," they had written.

"Schwyz has acted. Kaiser is dead. Will we follow through with our threat?" demanded a councilman.

"It is no longer possible for Zurich to fight Schwyz alone," answered a fellow council member. As he spoke again he looked down, thumbing through his stack of papers. "The other cantons of the confederacy have been gathering allies in anticipation of our attack…"

"Or to finally smash their Protestant enemies!" interrupted one of his colleagues.

The previous speaker continued. "The Catholic cantons have signed a pact with King Ferdinand; they will have the support of Austria, Bohemia, and Hungary. They have also rejected our demand that they disband these foreign allegiances."

He finally found the paper he was seeking. "We have it on good authority that Austria will send sixty companies of soldiers plus mounts and artillery to defend any Catholic cantons attacked by Protestants."

"We, too, have our allies," reminded another man. "Berne, Constance, and others will help us."

"Be careful about Berne, gentleman," urged Roust. "I fear that sleeping bear will fight only if provoked. She should not be depended on." Roust slid from his own stack of papers a folded letter from the now-Protestant canton. The black bear on the simplified coat of arms pressed into the red wax seal looked tame, nearly comical with its long tongue curling out of its open chops.

He began to read, "'God's Word calls only for peace and unity. You cannot really bring faith by means of spears and halberds.' Perhaps Berne is right. If they are not right, at least they seem firm. If we fight, we will do so alone."

Thus far, all the speakers had spoken from their seats. Finally, Ulrich rose to his feet. His words came almost through clenched teeth. "At this ripe moment, men, peace is war, and war is peace." Ulrich paused, fully expecting the surprised looks and raised eyebrows of the council. For as long as they had known him, he had preached mercilessly *against* the evils of warfare. "It is time," he continued, "for Christian soldiers to march against the armies of anti-Christ, not for money or vainglory, but to give free movement to the gospel!"

From the leather bag leaning against his chair, Ulrich produced a small stack of loose-leaf papers, neatly tied with a string, bearing the hand-written title, *Advice about the War*. "I too know a little of warfare, generals," he declared. "Scripture does not merely teach us how to pray. It also teaches our hands to make war."[1] The brand new, unpublished book scudded across the table until they bumped into the burgomaster's papers.

Ulrich's speech was strong. The reaction in the room was weak.

Burgomaster Roust could not forget the piles of dead Zurichers whom he had led to their graves in the disastrous Battle of Marignano almost fifteen years earlier. "I urge that we wait, and see what develops," he said, almost pleading.

Ulrich, still standing, clenched his fists under his black scholar's gown, his breathing now audible.

"Then you shall do it without me as your pastor," he threatened. "I will not stand by while God's servants are butchered for preaching the gospel, when we have the means to protect them."

Grabbing his bag, he stormed toward the door.

Burgomaster Roust tumbled his chair backwards, as he beat his friend to the exit. The pastor and mayor locked eyes.

"We *will* read your book," he said sternly, "*You* will continue to *preach* and *pray*. In ten days, when our emotions have stabilized, we will convene to make a final decision." The burgomaster paused before stating, with a careful balance of warmth and firmness, "I am thankful that you have a quick but short-lived temper, my friend."

---

1. Psalm 18:34

Ten days later, the news raced through the busy city streets: Zurich had declared war on the Catholic cantons!

The ranks of men that filed out of the city gates the next day—some forty companies— might not have looked like an army. Due to Ulrich's preaching against war, there were no longer many professional soldiers in Zurich and no matching uniforms. But since childhood, the men of Switzerland had learned to wield native weapons with frightening precision.

"Anna," persuaded her battle-ready husband, as he sat on the stone hearth with his three children draping his legs, "I suspect the battle will be waged without much bloodshed. Austria has reneged on its promise to protect her Catholic allies. You will see me alive and well by the month's end."

"But what about Roust's orders, that you keep your post in the church here in Zurich?" she responded, trying another tack to keep her husband home. "He has warned, and you must agree, that if the enemy reaches you, you will die."

"Roust knows that when my brethren expose their lives, I will not remain quiet at home," he replied. "Besides, I will do plenty of preaching to the men who have left their homes to face the foe. Save your tears, children, for a truly sad day!"

With that, he kissed his little family and entered the thronging streets. Before joining the march, he dropped a sealed envelope on the desk of the town clerk. The outside read, "To the wise and courageous lords of Berne." When the lords of Berne would open the letter—by then they would have heard of Zurich's declaration of war—they would read this:

"Be firm and do not fear war. True peace often comes through conflict. I do not thirst for anyone's blood, nor will I drink it even in case of tumult. My goal is to clip the wings of the oligarchs of Rome. Fear nothing, for we shall so manage all things with the goodness and the alliance of God that you shall not be ashamed or displeased because of us."

Leaving the clerk's office, Ulrich mounted his horse, situated his sword and battle-ax, and joined the march.

"The enemy has encamped at Kappel." The rumor which had circulated among the ranks of soldiers was now confirmed by their own eyes as they descended from the dense forest through which they had marched into the gently downward sloping valley.

Smoke curled from a dozen fires into the clear blue sky. Soon they could see soldiers milling between fires and tents. The sharp twangs of blacksmiths' hammers were the first sounds the approaching soldiers heard.

The Zurich men quickened their pace. Generals rode between their troops, shouting last minute orders.

Abruptly, the serpentine line halted. Those in the front of the line could see a single mounted horse racing up the ancient cow path toward the Zurich army. Breathless, the rider dismounted as he met the commander of the Protestant troops.

"My lord," said the rider, the burgomaster of a more neutral canton. "Your enemy is prepared to fight, but would prefer peace. Meet with them and resolve this conflict, without leading brother against brother."

Ulrich, who had rode to the front as he saw the rider approaching, heard the speech. With a jerk on the reigns, his horse side-stepped close to the Zurich general. "General," hissed Ulrich into the man's ear, "Do not listen to this false prophet. He would not be here if we were the weaker army."

Unmoved, the general told the visitor, "We will set up camp and parlay this evening. War might yet be prevented."

Turning his horse back to the messenger, Ulrich thrust out his sword while his horse tramped anxiously, champing against the tightened bit. "You will answer to God for this," he barked. "A weak and unprepared enemy always speaks fairly. You plead with us and urge us to make peace. Know this: when the enemy is fully armed he will not spare us and you will not be here, waving a white flag of truce."

"I believe that God will make all things well," returned the messenger, hastily mounting his horse.

Over the next several days, Ulrich wrote to Burgomaster Roust and his city council. "Don't be fooled by the sweet words of those we now have pinned to the ground. If you *must* make peace, be sure it is worth the price."

True to the promise he made to Anna, Ulrich busied himself by preaching to the waiting army. The thought rarely left his mind: "Who knows how many of these men will soon stand before God?" As the negotiations continued, Ulrich could not help noticing how the Catholic army continued to grow. At first, it was 9,000. Soon it was closer to 12,000. At the same time, the Protestant army was losing strength. The 5,000 man Berne army withdrew when it seemed that the Catholics would not attack.

In fact, peace began to seem more desirable. Strangely, the opposing armies, camped so near each other, were getting along wonderfully.

One night, Ulrich sat in his tent in front of a makeshift writing table. He smiled and rocked back on his stool as he recalled one of the highlights of the day.

Their Catholic "enemies" had dragged to the battle line a large wooden tub of cooked milk. "It's not much good without bread," one of the men had shouted into the Protestant camp. One of the Zurichers hollered back, "Our bread is a bit crunchy without milk." Soon, the more adventurous soldiers from both sides had gathered around the tub—being careful to observe the imaginary boundary line that divided the wooden tub as it sat between the two camps—and spooned out the warm milk-soggy bread. If anyone crossed the border, his enemy would be sure to slap a wooden spoon on his wrist.

"The fighting has been … mild," wrote Ulrich, "like children jousting for the biggest slice of pie on the family table. I can admit to you, dear wife, that I am glad we have signed a peace treaty today. Our opponents will pay all costs of the 'war' and provide suitable compensation for Jacob Kaiser's widow. They have also dissolved their union with Austria; my own eyes saw the document return to the dust of the earth. They are to cease from persecuting religious minorities, as are we." Remembering the words he had heard on the march, he added with a smile, "God makes all things well, even when our plans differ."

He folded the letter and tucked it in his coat pocket.

Around a nearby campfire, men had gathered around a lute player. Their voices, some trained to stick to the notes, others haphazardly roaming the scales, lifted old Swiss folk tunes into the dark summer sky. As one song gave way to the croaking and chirping of a million frogs and crickets, Ulrich nodded in the direction of the musician. Honored, the lutist handed his pastor the instrument. Ulrich picked and strummed for a few moments, then he opened his mouth to sing a song he had just written.

> Lord, guide the chariot of your fight.
> Our senses guide us wrong.
> Deliver us from sin's dark night,
> And all our rivals strong.

> Lord, raise your voice, proclaim your name
> Revive your troubled sheep.
> Lift up your arm and bring to shame
> Those who your will don't keep.
>
> God be our help, cause peace to reign
> In this confed'racy.
> Send us with joy from this campaign
> To all eternity.

As the song ended, a gunshot shattered the semi-silence of the sleepy camp. The heads around the fire swiveled toward the sound. "Probably just an excited Zuricher firing off a celebratory round," suggested a soldier. Still, Ulrich winced. Almost unvoluntarily, he said to himself, "This is an omen of a coming war which will not end in peace."

Family Skirmishes

The stream of burgundy wine glistened briefly in the light of the table candles before cascading into deep wooden cups. As usual, the Zwinglis' home was warm, not only from the summer heat, but also with lively conversation. The merry voices of her parents and their friends had just lulled little Regula to sleep in her small bedroom, down the hall from the dining room.

"Friends, I have a little news that might interest you," offered Ulrich, with a playful twinkle in his eye. To build suspense, he took a long sip from his cup. Then another.

"After years of sparring with pen and ink, I'm going to wrestle face to face with Doctor Luther. I just received the letter today from the German prince, Philip of Hesse. He's also invited Luther's right-hand man Philip Melanchthon and our dear Oecolampadius. It will be a conference to unite all German-speaking Christians by settling our disagreements once and for all."

Enthusiastic congratulations sounded around the table.

One of the Zurich theological students, however, was less confident. "Do you really think you can persuade Luther to agree to a common doctrine with us, especially on the Lord's Supper?" Wanting to impress his teacher, he ventured on. "Luther will not relent. For him, our Lord must be bodily present in Holy Communion. He thinks Christ can be held in a mug!" The student's finger flicked the wooden cup.

"You are right. I cannot persuade him," answered Ulrich, "But God's Word can, though perhaps Luther is too weak to listen."

"I've heard Luther called a lot of things," said Myconius, "But never weak."

"Consider this good strong wine," suggested Ulrich, swirling the drink around the sides of the cup. "To the healthy, it tastes excellent. It makes him merry, strengthens him, and warms his blood. But if there is someone who is sick of a disease or fever, he cannot even taste it, let alone drink it, and he marvels that the healthy is able to do so. This is not due to any defect in the wine, but to that of the sickness." To confirm his own good health, Ulrich took another swallow. "So too it is with the Word of God. It is right in itself and its proclamation is always for good. If there are those who cannot bear or understand to receive it, it is because they are sick."

"Then let's hope Luther is well," joked Myconius, "Because he's about to be served a barrel of the finest Zurich wine!"

Ulrich did not share with his company, or even with his wife, that the conference would be held in Marburg, Germany, more than 250 dangerous miles north. He also failed to mention that earlier that day, the burgomaster and his closest advisors had flatly denied his request to travel to the conference.

Two months later, three hours after sunset, he slipped out of his house, telling his wife that he would be going only a short distance on business. Twenty-three days later, Ulrich and his companions reached Marburg, accompanied by forty cavalry men sent from Prince Philip. Along the way the preacher had sent letters to Zurich, apologizing to the city council for leaving without their permission. "Please tell my dear wife," he had also written, "Whatever ought to be said to a woman in such a situation. I have tried to spare her the agonies of knowing that her husband is so far from the protection of his city."

That night, lying in a strange bed in a faraway castle, Ulrich's overloaded mind kept him awake. He fondly recalled the elation he had felt earlier that day as for the first time he had talked face to face with the most famous Protestant in the world. He loved and admired Luther and had always done his best to see that his books circulated in Switzerland. If he wrote or spoke harshly against Luther, it was for political reasons. Lutheranism was a heresy in the Holy Roman Empire. Ulrich had enough problems of his own without being associated with another "heretic."

But as he tried harder to fall asleep, heavier, less happy thoughts entered his mind. For two years he had been working hard to forge alliances between the scattered reforming communities in Switzerland, France, and Germany. Without agreement, the reformed church could easily be crushed by the powerful Catholic Church. Would the next few days bring unity, or only widen the divide?

Just before drifting off, he happily recalled listening to his own father, a local politician and Christian man, share his experiences around the evening fire. "In politics, as in life," he had once told his family, "never forget to recall what you have in common with your opponent. Extend a brotherly hand. If you speak like a friend, you might just gain one."

The next morning, a tired Ulrich entered the magnificent debate hall. Six-sided stone columns supported a beautifully plastered arched ceiling. Luther and his colleagues were already seated around a large wooden table, draped with a gold-tasseled red cloth. Ulrich smiled affectionately at the admired theologian. Luther seemed to interpret his smile as a sign of pride; his face hardened.

Ulrich, Oecolampadius, and several scholarly friends took their seat at another table when Prince Philip entered the room. Slowly, the room's echoes subsided as the guests prepared to listen to Philip's greeting. Instead, from Luther's table came the distinct sounds of tapping and scratching. He was writing words onto his table with a stick of chalk. Though the words were upside down and across the room, Ulrich could not mistake them.

Hoc est corpus meum.

(This is my body.)

"So," thought Ulrich, "The whole debate will hinge on these four words of Christ, from Mark 14:22. How can Luther not understand that when Christ said these words, he was indicating that the bread he held in his hand *signified* his body? Jesus never taught that the bread of the Lord's Supper turned into his body. Luther will never budge!"

Moments later, Luther rose to his feet and confirmed Ulrich's fears. "I disagree with my adversaries about the presence of Christ in the supper. And I will always disagree with them. Nothing they can say will change my mind. I reject reason, common sense, arguments, and evidence. God has spoken."

For two days, disagreement deepened. Luther seemed to become colder by the hour. Deeply grieved, Ulrich wept.

Both sides had also heard whispering among the court that a deadly plague had descended upon the city outside the castle. How long would it take before it found its way in? Everyone seemed eager to return home.

"Good men of God," pleaded Philip, "I implore you, do not leave until you have done your very best to agree on what you can. Meet one more time, tomorrow morning. I charge Dr. Luther to call to mind the kindness of Christ, and to write a document outlining your shared convictions. You will do your best to agree to that document tomorrow, then you may leave."

The next morning, the two sides easily agreed on the first fourteen of fifteen propositions. They could not quite agree on the last. Though they could say this: "We agree that the sacrament of the altar is the sacrament of the very body and very blood of Jesus Christ, and that the spiritual eating of this body and blood is especially necessary to every Christian in order to strengthen our weak faith. We cannot yet agree about how Christ is present in the supper, but toward that end we will work with prayer and charity."

Most of the Zwingli family was too young to tell that the head of the household was discouraged by the failed Marburg Conference; Regula now had a three-year-old brother, William, and a one-year-old baby brother, Ulrich, who was named after their father. The always-confident pastor was as committed as ever to the cause of reformation, but his wife and close friends could not possibly fail to notice that he was unusually heavy-hearted. He still found time to pour out his soul with his music. But less often now would he sing the catchy, familiar folk songs of his childhood. More than ever he was "Psalm-making," singing like the war-tempered, family-betrayed, enemy-encompassed King David. Still, his children loved to hear their father's melodic voice and watch his nimble fingers draw music from his old lute. And he loved to see their eyes twinkle as they watched him.

"Regula, my fingers are starting to wiggle," he said one evening as he slid his chair back from the table after supper.

Regula clapped her chubby five-year-old hands as she stared at her papa's. His right hand began to strum the air while his left hand slowly—then more rapidly—fingered imaginary frets.

"Do you think you could fetch…"

But he had no need to finish. Regula raced to the wall where Ulrich's lute hung from two wooden pegs.

"Do you have a new song for us, Papa?" she asked.

Her father's eyes were closed as he instinctively tuned the fifteen strings. The flicks of sound from the familiar instrument brought a smile to Anna's face as she swirled a wet dishrag around a wooden plate.

"The song is not jovial. But its truth can make you very happy, dear daughter." He smiled as he looked into Regula's eager face.

> Lord, we cry to you for help.
> Only you can heal our pain.
> Out of deep distress we call.
> Help us, Lord, send peace again.

As Ulrich strummed on, he gently bit his lips together as he felt the pain of a divided nation, a divided church, a divided reformation. He felt like a less muscular Hercules, who for a time carried the burden of the world on his shoulders. But he also remembered Christ's promise to always hear his people's prayer as he ruled in the midst of his enemies.[1] With eyes closed, he sang on.

> We have sinned against your law.
> We have failed to do your will,
> Disobeyed your holy word.
> Lord, have mercy on us still.
>
> Purge our souls of selfishness.
> Cleanse our hearts of bitterness.
> Lead us back to righteousness.
> Save us, Lord, O save us still.

Again, he worked the strings, up and down the wide fret board, while he meditated with closed jaw. "I have poured my life into this work. How easy it is for me to be selfish in my prayers for 'Ulrich's reformation.' I also know bitterness. How I can loathe those who pour water on the flame of true religion. I need your salvation, Lord!"

As he approached the final stanza, he quickened his strumming; music tumbled loudly from the instrument.

> Lord, exalt your holy name.
> Conquer evil by your power.
> Let your righteous will prevail.
> Reign victorious ever more.

---

1. Psalm 110:2.

As the last strong note left his mouth, he slapped his hand across the soundboard. The room was suddenly silent, save for the fire's soft crackling.

But not for long.

Regula began clapping her hands until her father scooped her up in his strong arm. He placed the lute on its pegs and his daughter in her bed, with an affectionate kiss on her forehead.

The Second Kappel War

"My dear Vadian."

After penning the name of his beloved friend, Ulrich returned the quill to its stand. He closed his eyes. His nostrils drew in a long draft of the warm summer air. He bent his head backward, articulating every vertebrae of his creaky spine. As he exhaled, slowly and deeply, he felt a little life return to his troubled soul. He resumed writing.

"God brought both of us into this world forty-seven years ago. As young men we could never have guessed that God would have us in the middle of a great revival of the Christian faith. You know that the gospel of grace is gaining strength in Switzerland, Germany, and many other regions throughout Europe. But it has not come without a price. I am weary of fighting with those who should be our friends. The Empire wants to crush us, as do the Catholic cantons. You know how I loathe warfare. But you will see that unless we first strike a decisive blow against the Catholics, or dissolve the Swiss confederacy entirely, there will never be peace among us. Instead—I hate to say it—we have taken the worst course possible. Despite my vehement opposition, the counselors from Berne persuaded the reformed cities to prevent all wheat, wine, salt, iron, and steel from entering the lands of our opponents until they change their view. What a cowardly act! We will starve our brothers—and their wives and children—rather than engage them in manly combat. But this crushes my soul; the common opinion is that this is Zwingli's embargo, though I hate it more than all men. Vadian, I cannot go on. Tomorrow I will resign as gospel minister of my beloved Great Minster. Your teary-eyed friend, Ulrich."

Over the next several days, Ulrich pleaded with the council to release him of his duties. "For too long I have borne a too-heavy burden of preaching and teaching," he insisted. "I am sick in body, and discouraged in soul. How long will you make me go on?"

The council was firm. "You must remain at your post to see things through to the end!"

As the days passed, nearly every conversation seemed to touch on the war that lurked around the corner. Signs of war seemed even to paint the sky.

"What do you make of it, Master Ulrich?" asked a reformed minister. The two men were surrounded by a growing crowd in the stone courtyard behind the Great Minster. The last light of the setting sun showed fear on the faces that gazed into the heavens. What they saw was a pale-yellow comet—later to be known as

Halley's Comet—a dull , star-like shape, stretching its long tail through the sky.

"Sir," answered Ulrich, "It will cost me and many an honest man his life, and truth and church will yet suffer."

"So, it is an omen of great evil," confirmed the man.

"Even so," concluded Ulrich, "Christ will not desert us."

* * *

It was early on the morning of October 11, 1531. The city of Zurich was frantic with activity. An angry and hungry army of several thousand Catholics had crossed into the Zurich canton two days earlier. Now, men, horses, and cannon, crisscrossed the dew-covered cobblestones. Wives and children embraced their husbands and fathers amidst tears and last goodbyes. Women held their children in their doorways; more courageous children ventured into the streets.

Ulrich too had bid farewell to his young family. Regula's screams—"Papa!"—still rattled through his helmet as his horse cantered out of the city.

Ulrich's chain mail shirt jingled with each step of his horse. "My God, we will never return!" he said to himself as he passed some abandoned cannon which had been discarded when not enough horses could be found to pull them. The ill-equipped soldiers he passed looked up when they heard Ulrich praying aloud as he rode.

"You had better pray!" jeered some of the Zurichers, many of whom had always despised his reformation.

"Before day's end, you will stand before God with our blood on your hands. How will you protest then?"

Tears blurred Ulrich's vision.

Between prayers, and tears, he remembered.

He easily recalled the pain of his father's firm spankings from almost half a century earlier. Always, the father's strong arms would embrace him during discipline, assuring his son of his steadfast love. "Again my Father is disciplining me for my sin. I have depended too much on the powers of men. I have forgotten about the power of God's Word. Let me not squirm out of this discipline now," he prayed, "But embrace his rebukes as from a loving and wise Father."

How often had he and his brothers staged mock-battles in the grassy hills of Wildhaus? War then was always so glamorous. The good confederates had always repelled the invading armies. The "slain" warriors had always picked themselves out of the grass when their mothers had called them in for supper. One of his favorite lines from his now-estranged friend Erasmus crossed his lips: "War is exciting only for those who have never known its misery." The chaplain of the Zurich army was almost overtaken by despondency.

Suddenly, the rattling armor of his hopeless army brought to mind words he had memorized years ago, as he was copying St. Paul's epistles into his own notebook from Erasmus' Greek New Testament.

"Finally, my brethren, be strong in the Lord and in the power of his might. Put on the whole armor of God, that you may be able to stand against the wiles of the devil. For we do not wrestle against flesh and blood, but against principalities, against powers, against the rulers of the darkness of this age, against spiritual hosts of wickedness in the heavenly places. Therefore take up the whole armor of God, that you may be able to withstand in the evil day, and having done all, to stand."[1]

Ulrich's horse lurched, surprised by its rider's voice now shouting near his ears. "Men, this is our evil day. The battle which will shortly commence may be so heated that he who rests for a moment will be destroyed. Be sober. Be vigilant. Your enemy will prowl about you, seeking to devour you. Listen to my words: Quit you like men, be strong."[2]

By this time, all of the soldiers who could hear him were listening intently.

"Do you not hear in these words, brothers, our calling also as Christians? The Christian life is a battle, so sharp and full of danger that effort can nowhere be relaxed without loss. We know not how God will decide the conflict on this sacred ground today. Many of us may not be standing in the flesh by nightfall. And yet we can stand in God's power. The Christian life is always a lasting victory, for he who fights wins, if he remains loyal to Christ the head. My brothers, listen to Saint Paul. 'For if we live, we live to the Lord; and if we die, we die to

---

1. Ephesians 6:10-13
2. 1 Corinthians 16:13; KJV

the Lord. Therefore, whether we live or die, we are the Lord's.'"[3]

Amidst the spontaneous praying and preaching of their minister, the ragtag army of only a few thousand untrained and disorganized men marched out of step into the heat of the day. Before noon, the Zurich army crested the range of hills that separated the city from the battlefield.

Again, their spirits sank.

Greatly outnumbered, the several hundred Zurich troops which had deployed the previous day had dug in on high ground. But they were nearly trapped from behind by a water-filled ditch and surrounded by marsh. Between them and their vast enemy was a forest, which could easily cover a surprise attack by the Catholics.

"We should wait here until more reinforcements come from Zurich," one of the generals suggested. "The numbers are certainly against us."

"Dear sir," argued Ulrich, "We cannot sit here while our fellows are dug in to fight. If the attack begins, will we watch the slaughter as one watches a play? We must move into position. Perhaps we were fools to not make peace when we could. But our enemies will now settle for nothing but blood. They will attack. We must not shrink back now when our friends need us most. To talk in glowing terms of bravery when danger is far away, is weak and despicable; but to be steadfast and

---

3. Romans 14:8

undeterred when confronted with danger, that is the only sign of a brave heart."

The troops marched on.

By mid-afternoon, the uneven battle began. It was short. Soon the road back to Zurich was crawling with the wounded and deserting.

Those who would never return to their home littered the marsh grass. A few small groups of resolute soldiers continued to fight a losing battle. Among these, lingering to shout encouragements to his brave friends, was the most famous gospel minister in the country. The Catholic army swarmed the remaining Protestant soldiers until none were left standing.

As dusk descended on the muddy battle swamp, Ulrich Zwingli, leaned against a small bush, breathing heavily. He fought to remain conscious. His legs were thrust through with spears. His helmet and skull were crushed by a large rock. Ulrich pressed his hands to his forehead as pain rippled down his face. He drew his hands back in front of his eyes; blood streamed down his wrists.

His thoughts were drawn to his beloved Savior. An ancient chant with ancient words sang through his mind:

O sacred Head, now wounded,
With grief and shame weighed down,
Now scornfully surrounded
With thorns, Thine only crown;
O sacred Head, what glory,
What bliss till now was thine!

> Yet, though despised and gory,
> I joy to call Thee mine.

In the chaos—blasting muskets, groaning men, screaming horses, mud-slurping boots tromping through the marsh, pain, loss of blood—the suffering of Christ seemed to mingle with Ulrich's suffering. As never before, if only for a moment, he understood Jesus' words: Deny yourself, take up your cross, follow me. Do not fear to lose the world if you gain your soul—nothing is as valuable![4]

With his last strength he voiced his victory: "They can kill the body, but not the soul!"

---

4. Mark 8:34-36

Afterword

Ulrich Zwingli's death seemed to be a tremendous victory for his enemies. When his body was discovered on the battlefield the next morning, it was cut into four pieces and then burned: the traditional punishment for treason and heresy.

His dear widow Anna mourned not only for her husband but also for a son from her previous marriage, who fell not far from his beloved stepfather. In the same brief battle, she also lost a brother, a son-in-law, and a brother-in-law.

For his friends, Ulrich's death provided a sad but necessary rebuke of the use of fleshly force in the cause of God. Oecolampadius and Myconius, two of Ulrich's dearest friends, felt in their loss God's gracious discipline. "It is time for us to trust more in God's gospel and less in the strength of man," they said.

Ulrich was succeeded as pastor by twenty-seven-year-old Heinrich Bullinger, who, just three years earlier, had participated in the Berne Conference, along with his mentor. Bullinger would pastor the

Great Minster for more than forty years. He was a careful thinker who was able to refine much of Ulrich's rushed thought into more mature and careful theology. Ulrich's ideas can be clearly seen in one of Bullinger's most enduring works, *The Second Helvetic Confession* (1561), which still guides many reformed believers to this day.

Appendix:
Religious Use of Violence during the Reformation

It is impossible to ignore the fact that during the sixteenth century, as in all centuries before and after, religious and irreligious people sometimes resorted to the use of force in promoting their ideas.

Roman Catholic historians suggest that their church burned between 4,000 and 40,000 religious opponents between the years 1480 and 1800. In those years the Roman Church imposed severe penalties upon hundreds of thousands. Non-Catholics too, sometimes used fear and force to suppress their critics. Sadly, this was true in Ulrich Zwingli's city of Zurich. Not only did the Zurich city council preside over several executions of people who disagreed with the reforming church, Zwingli himself provided little space for religious disagreement. Baptists and Catholic monks and nuns were treated with inexcusable harshness by those who had adopted reformation doctrine. When a majority of people in a region decided for the reformation, the Catholic minority was denied rights and sometimes forced to leave. Zwingli did not allow others the liberty of conscience which he valued so highly.

Throughout history, the people of God have often forgotten about his means for enlarging his kingdom. So how do we come to terms with the fact that some of our "heroes" wrongly used violence in an attempt to promote the cause of Christ?

1. *We should try to understand our heroes' faults, but not defend them.* When we consider the heroes of the faith in Hebrews 11, we are struck by this reality: Our great cloud of witnesses includes those who struggled with drunkenness (Noah), anger (Moses), and sexual purity (Samson). Our heroes have been polygamists (Abraham), deceivers (Jacob), and doubters (Sarah). Scripture is shockingly honest about believers' sins in order that we might take heed, lest we fall into the same sins (1 Corinthians 10:13). To be a godly example, one need not be perfect, only sincere in following God in the face of challenges. Ulrich Zwingli was a sinner saved by grace. We need not, and we must not, defend his sins, in order to be grateful for his life.

2. *God's people are seduced by the sins of their age.* The patriarchs could hardly imagine what we now take for granted; godly marriages—the kind that reflect God's will before sin entered the world—are made by the lifelong union of one man and one woman. The generation of Israelites who left Egypt were pressed hard by the temptation to complain against God. Many godly men of the nineteenth century held

regrettable views regarding evolution and slavery. Generations from now, church historians will lament some of our current views and practices. In the sixteenth century, almost no one could conceive of the peaceful coexistence of people with strongly held opposing beliefs. Heresy, or serious doctrinal error, was considered by almost all sixteenth century people to be an offense worthy of death. We should not be surprised that Ulrich Zwingli spoke harshly against his opponents and urged the use of harsh measures against them.

3. *Godly people often believe better than they behave.* God's people in this life are both sinners and saints. We hold biblical principles but fail to see how they should be applied in every area. We teach truth but struggle to live truth. And we often fail to see the contradictions of our own lives. Zwingli was at his best when he stuck to one of his leading principles: Change comes by clear teaching and principled decisions. Sadly, Zwingli tarnished the gospel when his zeal for the reformation muddied his confidence that God's kingdom advances not by human, but by divine power worked through proper means.

We should be honest about the faults of our heroes. We should grieve over them. We should learn from them. But we should not be discouraged from imitating those flawed believers who have gone before us insofar as they teach us to imitate Christ (1 Corinthians 11:1).

Ulrich Zwingli:
Timeline

1483	Martin Luther is born in Germany.
1484	Ulrich Zwingli is born in Wildhaus, Switzerland.
1489-1498	Zwingli studies in Weesen, Basel, and Berne.
1492	Christopher Columbus discovers the New World.
1498-1506	Zwingli studies at the universities of Vienna and Basel.
1506-1516	Zwingli pastors at Glarus.
1508-1512	Michelangelo paints the Sistine Chapel ceiling.
1509	Future Swiss reformer, John Calvin, is born.
1512, 1515	Zwingli serves as chaplain with Swiss fighters at Milan and Marignano.
c. 1516	Zwingli visits Erasmus in Basel.
1516-1518	Zwingli pastors at Einsiedeln.
1517	The Reformation begins in Germany.
1519-1556	Charles V reigns over Holy Roman Empire.
1519-1531	Zwingli pastors the Great Minster Church at Zurich.
1522	Zwingli writes against forced fasting following the affair of the sausages.
1523-1524	Three theological disputations are held in Zurich.
1524	Zwingli and Anna Reinhart marry and their firstborn child, Regula, is born.
1524	Zurich council purges images from the churches.
1524-1525	Peasants' War rages in Germany.

1525	Conrad Grebel officiates the first "rebaptism" in Zurich.
1525	Zwingli first serves the Lord's Supper after the reformed manner
1526	Zwingli's son William is born; Baden Conference is held.
1528	Ulrich Zwingli Jr. is born while Zwingli participates in the Berne disputation.
1529	Austria defeats the Ottoman Empire in Vienna.
1529	First War of Kappel is avoided by a treaty.
1529	Zwingli participates in the Marburg Colloquy with Martin Luther.
1531	Zurich enforces a food blockade against the Catholic cantons.
1531	Ulrich Zwingli dies at Kappel.
1531-1532	The Church of England recognizes the king, not the Pope, as head of the church.

Ulrich Zwingli: Life Summary

Ulrich Zwingli was a Swiss religious reformer and social activist who lived from 1484-1531. Just seven weeks after the birth of Martin Luther, Zwingli—who is sometimes called the "third man of The Reformation"—was born in a small village nestled in the Swiss Alps. In Zwingli's early years he received a rigorous classical education, which would later give him the ability to understand the spiritual problems of his day and the skills to work for biblical change in the church.

While still a Roman Catholic, Zwingli pastored two small Swiss congregations before accepting the call to lead one of the most significant churches in Switzerland, the Great Minster Church in Zurich. In Zurich, Zwingli preached, taught, and sometimes acted as a foreign diplomat, in addition to caring for a wife and family. He restarted the early church practice of expository preaching—or preaching through the Bible chapter by chapter, explaining and applying the Scriptures to the people. His preaching was popular because it was accessible, bold, witty, and biblical. At the same time, Zwingli preached tirelessly against the Swiss practice of mercenary soldiering. As he matured, he would also oppose Catholic ceremonies and the church's unbiblical tyranny of conscience. After leading a large number of believers and churches out of the Roman Catholic Church, Zwingli worked hard, though largely unsuccessfully, to build a Protestant consensus with both princes and theologians, most notably with Martin Luther.

Not surprisingly, he soon developed enemies, not only within the Catholic Church, but also among his own students. Some of his more radical followers, whom he labeled "Anabaptists" (or rebaptizers), felt he was too careful in his reform and quickly formed their own religious sects. As the religious reformation developed, it also brought great unrest among the Swiss states. By the end of the 1530s, Zwingli's State of Zurich had become largely isolated from the rest of the mostly Catholic confederacy. In 1531, a sort of cold war flared into a heated civil war. Serving as a citizen-chaplain, Zwingli was killed in a brief war on October 11, 1531.

Thinking Further Topics

The Birth of a Warrior
Ulrich Zwingli's father told his boys the story of William Tell so that they could better understand where they came from. Tell's story is part of their story. How can telling the great stories of God's redemption in Scripture help believers to feel more a part of God's story? (See Exodus 12:26-27; Psalm 78).

The Shaping of a Scholar-Shepherd
Have you ever wondered why children need to be educated? Seventeenth century poet John Milton suggested that children should be educated in order to prepare them for private and public service, as well as to "repair the ruins of our first parents by regaining to know God aright, and out of that knowledge to love Him, to be like Him, as we may the nearest by possessing our soul of true virtue." Do you think Zwingli could have been a reformer had he not been diligent in his studies? What does Proverbs 4:1-13 say about the need for you to get wisdom?

Field Preacher

You read about Zwingli's strong opposition to non-defensive warfare. The Bible acknowledges that there is a "time of war, and a time of peace" (Ecclesiastes 3:8). But it also warns against our sinful tendency to "fight and war" to satisfy our fleshly desires (James 4:1-2). Paul also admonishes believers to lead a quiet life and to mind their own business (1 Thessalonians 4:11). In what ways is war glorified today? How can you, as a child, learn from Zwingli's opposition to mercenary soldiering?

A Step Closer to Zurich

As a young man, Ulrich Zwingli failed to remain sexually pure. Read in Proverbs 7 about Solomon's warning to young men—he writes to "my son." Keep in mind that Solomon tragically failed to keep his own counsel. The Bible says that "King Solomon loved many foreign women...his wives turned his heart after other gods; and his heart was not loyal to the LORD his God" (1 Kings 11:1, 4). For his physical and spiritual adultery, God tore the kingdom of Israel in half. What kind of consequences might young people today face for sexual immorality?

First Year in Zurich

Ulrich Zwingli was, at times, so committed to his work that he failed to care for his health. We too, can fail to see care of our bodies as an important Christian discipline. Notice how Jesus takes an interest in the physical well-being of his disciples in Mark 6:31-32. The disciples were tired and hungry, busy with their ministry. But Jesus helped them to see that disciples are not just spirits, but bodies too. How might you better care for your body?

Of Meat and Marriage

In the church of Jesus Christ, there seems to be no limit to the ways that believers can offend each other. In Zwingli's day, some believers were offended that they could not eat meat during Lent. Others were offended when people did eat meat. What are some of the issues upon which Christians seem to disagree today, and over which people seem to become offended? How can Paul's words in Romans 14 help Christians live in greater peace, despite differing convictions?

The Great Debater

The word "debate" sounds very negative to many people today. On hearing the word, you might picture angry people insulting each other and arrogantly boasting in their own positions. Zwingli, along with many others in his day, firmly believed that truth could be reached by clearly contrasting one idea against another, particularly when these ideas found a home in Scripture. Read Mark 2:1-3:6 to see how Jesus skillfully debated his religious opponents. What can you learn from Jesus about interacting with those who disagree with you?

How does Jude 22-23 help us understand the different approaches we should take in debates, depending on our opponents?

New Radicals

Zwingli's goal was to bring about a careful and informed reformation. He believed that changes having to do with the essence of the Christian faith cannot wait. But he was convinced that change can also happen too rapidly. At the same time, he was clear that sinful traditions should not be tolerated forever. He agreed with Paul, who boasts that in the beginning he fed the Corinthians with milk because they could not handle meat. (1 Corinthians 3:2). Do you tend to be more cautious, like Zwingli, or more zealous, like the Anabaptists? Can you describe some scenarios in which cautious change is best? What about times when zealous leadership is necessary?

The End of the Mass

The first reformed celebration of the Lord's Supper in Zurich was a very special event. It was special for the adults who ate the bread and drank the wine. But it was also special for the children who were witnesses to this great event. In most churches that follow the customs of the Swiss reformers—Ulrich Zwingli and John Calvin—children of believers participate in the Lord's Supper only after publicly professing their faith before the elders and the congregation. In so doing, the elders are helping the young people to rightly examine themselves, to discern the Lord's body, and to judge themselves as worthy participants of the Lord's Supper (1 Corinthians 11:27-34). How can young people who have not yet professed their faith benefit from the Lord's Supper even if they are not served the bread and wine? To help answer that question, read Exodus 12:21-28 (especially verses 26-27) and see how children were to participate in the Passover (which preceded the Lord's Supper) by paying close attention to the ritual and by asking questions of their parents.

War of Water and Words

It is hard to imagine the harsh words and actions used between professing Christians during the sixteenth century (and at other times during church history). As you can read in the Appendix, we cannot defend such unchristian behavior as the drowning of Felix Manz. But it is important to try to understand why men went to such lengths to defend what they thought was right. Those who mistreat others in the name of Christianity often believe that they are fighting for God against those who are undermining God's reputation. The Zurich City Council, for example, would have a hard time understanding how some Christians in our day find it so easy to "agree to disagree." How do Ephesians 5:1, 2 and Ephesians 6:10-20 teach us to be both zealous for truth and loving toward our disagreeable neighbors?

The First Kappel War

Solomon famously wrote, "To everything there is a season, a time for every purpose under heaven...A time to love and a time to hate; a time of war, and a time of peace" (Ecclesiastes 3:1,8). Zwingli was naturally a peaceful man who hated the typical evils of warfare. But he also believed that there was a time for war. Looking back, we can criticize Zwingli and others for using the weapons of the flesh in a spiritual conflict. Still, Zwingli can help us to think about when we should make peace and when we should train our hands for war (Psalm 18:34). Can you think of examples in your life where you should make peace? Can you think of examples where you have entered into a conflict?

Family Skirmishes

The Marburg Conference is one of the most disappointing chapters of the Protestant Reformation. It is painful to imagine what lasting testimony of unity Luther and Zwingli might have given the church if they were able to unite their reform movements. The reasons for the failure are many and complex. Luther and Zwingli differed in their family backgrounds and their education. As Luther acknowledged at the conference, the two men had different spirits. At the same time, the conference probably failed for one simple reason: pride. Neither side was willing to give up what they wanted. James teaches us that we war and fight because we do not restrain our desire for gratification (James 4:1-5). Can you think of ways in which your desires fight against unity among your friends and family members? What is James' encouragement for prideful Christians? (v. 6).

The Second Kappel War

The Christian life is a battle. Christians fight strong foes: the world, the devil, and the flesh. We have been given spiritual armor and weapons: truth, righteousness, the gospel, faith, salvation, Scripture, and prayer (Ephesians 6:14-20). We follow a great Warrior who will make his enemy his footstool (Psalm 110:1) and lead his victorious followers into an eternal dwelling which he has purchased with his own blood. Ulrich Zwingli did not always choose the right battles. He did not always use the right weapons. But he does teach us to fight. He would have agreed with words Isaac Watts wrote almost 200 years after Zwingli's death: "Since I must fight if I would reign, increase my courage, Lord; I'll bear the toil, endure the pain, supported by Thy Word."

Either alone, or with your family, spend some time thinking about the spiritual battles that you have to fight. Then pray to that great Shepherd Warrior, Jesus Christ, for courage in the battle.

About the Author

William Boekestein is the pastor of Immanuel Fellowship Church in Kalamazoo, Michigan. In his free time he enjoys reading books with his wife Amy, and their four children. His family also loves to ride bikes and travel to new places.

He has authored three illustrated children's books on the reformed confessions:

Faithfulness under Fire: The Story of Guido de Bres,

The Quest for Comfort: The Story of the Heidelberg Catechism, and *The Glory of Grace:*

The Story of the Canons of Dort.

He has also written *Ulrich Zwingli* in EP Books' "Bitesize Biography" series.

You can email William at billboek@hotmail.com or follow him on Facebook and Twitter (@Williamboek).

OTHER BOOKS IN THE
TRAILBLAZERS SERIES

For a full list of Trailblazers, please see our
website: www.christianfocus.com
All Trailblazers are available as e-books

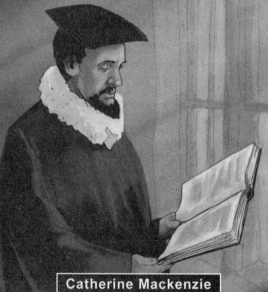

John Calvin: After Darkness Light
by Catherine Mackenzie

Calvin had ideas on how we could live better lives —
particularly how we could live in close harmony with
God and each other — but because his ideas were radical,
his life was filled with dramatic events and dangers. He
was run out of town — and then welcomed back. He
was accused of being too harsh — and also too tender
hearted. When he explained what the bible meant he
was considered too logical and too spiritual! He must
have been an amazing man to have caused such a stir!

ISBN: 978-1-178191-550-9

TRAIL BLAZERS
• Martin Luther•
REFORMATION FIRE
Catherine Mackenzie

Martin Luther: Reformation Fire
by Catherine Mackenzie

What made an ordinary monk become a catalyst for the Reformation in Europe in the 1500s? What were the reasons lying behind his nailing of 93 theses against the practice of indulgences to the door of the Schlosskirche in Wittenberg in 1517? Why was Martin Luther's life in danger? How did his apparent kidnapping result in the first ever New Testament translated into the German language? Discover how a fresh understanding of the Scriptures transformed not only his own life but had a huge impact upon Europe.

ISBN: 978-1-78191-521-9

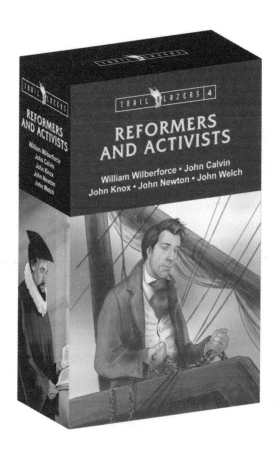

TRAIL BLAZERS 4

REFORMERS
AND ACTIVISTS

William Wilberforce • John Calvin
John Knox • John Newton • John Welch

Trailblazer Reformers and Activists Box Set 4

This giftbox collection of colourful trailblazer stories makes a perfect present that will delight young minds. Features some of the great Christian reformers and activists who will inspire young and old alike. This edition includes William Wilberforce, the man fought to bring freedom and relief from the terrors of the slave trade and John Knox, who went from being a bodyguard to a preacher of God's Word.

ISBN: 978-1-78191-637-7

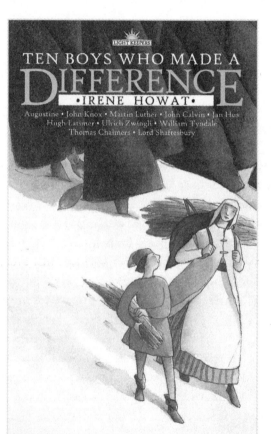

TEN BOYS WHO MADE A
DIFFERENCE
•IRENE HOWAT•

Augustine • John Knox • Martin Luther • John Calvin • Jan Hus
Hugh Latimer • Ulrich Zwingli • William Tyndale
Thomas Chalmers • Lord Shaftesbury

Ten Boys who Made a Difference
by Irene Howat

Would you like to make a difference? These ten boys grew up to do just that – but first they had to change the church. How did God change them?

Augustine discovered the love of God and changed the way we think; **Knox** focused on God's Word and told his country the truth; **Luther** rediscovered God's truth and gave it to ordinary people; **Calvin** realised that salvation was a gift from God and not a reward for what he did; **Tyndale** longed to print the Bible in a language that everyone would understand; **Latimer** urged people to read the Bible for themselves and made enemies as a result; **Hus** taught that God is in charge of the church and the world; **Zwingli** challenged people to obey God's Word in every area of their lives; **Chalmers** called the church to show Christ's compassion to the poor and **Shaftesbury** pushed the church into making Christ's love a living reality for everyone.

ISBN: 978-1-85792-775-7